WOMAN ON A MISSION

Katherine Bell Fraser in Armenia, 1892–1897

From Christian Missionary
to Refugee Advocate

Andria HILL-LEHR

NIMBUS
PUBLISHING
NIMBUS.CA

Nimbus Publishing Limited
3660 Strawberry Hill Street, Halifax, NS, B3K 5A9
(902) 455-4286 nimbus.ca

Printed and bound in Canada
NB1541

Editor: Marianne Ward
Cover design: Heather Bryan
Interior Design: Rudi Tusek

Library and Archives Canada Cataloguing in Publication

Title: Woman on a mission : Katherine Bell Fraser in Armenia, 1892-1897 : from Christian missionary to refugee advocate / Andria Hill-Lehr.
Names: Hill-Lehr, Andria, author.
Description: Includes bibliographical references and index.
Identifiers: Canadiana (print) 20210218061 | Canadiana (ebook) 20210218126 | ISBN 9781774710333 (softcover) ISBN 9781774710340 (EPUB)
Subjects: LCSH: Bell Fraser, Katherine, 1865-1899. | LCSH: Bell Fraser, Katherine, 1865-1899—Travel—Armenia. | LCSH: Armenian massacres, 1894-1896. | LCSH: Armenia—History—1801-1900. | LCSH: Armenia—Social conditions—19th century. | LCSH: Women missionaries—Nova Scotia—Biography. | LCSH: Women missionaries—Armenia—Biography. | LCSH: Human rights workers—Armenia—Biography. | LCSH: Women human rights workers—Armenia—Biography. | LCGFT: Biographies.
Classification: LCC DS194.5.B45 H55 2021 | DDC 956.6/20154092—dc23

Canada | Canada Council for the Arts / Conseil des arts du Canada | NOVA SCOTIA

Nimbus Publishing acknowledges the financial support for its publishing activities from the Government of Canada, the Canada Council for the Arts, and from the Province of Nova Scotia. We are pleased to work in partnership with the Province of Nova Scotia to develop and promote our creative industries for the benefit of all Nova Scotians.

FSC www.fsc.org MIX Paper from responsible sources FSC® C013916

To Ron Lehr,
with love and gratitude
for the support you have
always shown me

Acknowledgements

Thanks to the team at Nimbus Publishing and especially Marianne Ward, who guided this manuscript through its final edits.

Table of Contents

Introduction

One day in June 2005, while waiting in the Nova Scotia Archives for a box of research materials, my gaze wandered to the card catalogues lining one wall. In the days before internet search engines and computerized catalogues, this was how we looked for information. They offered a serendipitous, tactile opportunity to find something one isn't necessarily looking for. At least, that's how I sometimes used them, rather like when you open a book to a random page to seek guidance or an answer to a question—a bibliophile's divination. I scanned the labels on the drawer fronts. I can't now recall whether the label that caught my eye said "biography" or "people," but whichever it was, it evoked "story." I slid the drawer open, ran my fingertips lightly along the tops of the cards, and randomly selected one. On it was "Katherine Bell Fraser: papers of her missionary work in Armenia, 1892–1897." I recorded the call number in my notebook and returned some weeks later to see what was there. Two small archive boxes containing a few photographs, a journal, and almost two hundred letters drew me into a tale of travel, adventure, hardship, and atrocity, seen through the eyes of a young Nova Scotia woman who went to

Armenia as a missionary and then coordinated relief work for nine thousand Armenian refugees in Bulgaria—all before she turned thirty. In this book I quote extensively from Fraser's papers, letting stand her misspellings, lack of punctuation, and sentence fragments, all of which allow us to hear her voice and get a sense of the person behind this remarkable story.

Fraser's story is part of Canada's history of helping refugees, dating back to a time before there even was a "Canada" as we know it. According to the government website Canada: A History of Refuge, "freemen and slaves fleeing the oppression of the American Revolution" came north of the forty-ninth parallel in 1776. In contrast, Canada failed thousands of Jewish refugees fleeing a Europe in the thrall of Hitler's politics in the 1930s and tried to compensate for that lack of foresight and compassion by admitting 250,000 displaced persons in the aftermath of the Second World War. In the latter half of the twentieth century and early part of the twenty-first, we have found room for, among others, Vietnamese "boat people," Bosnians, Kosovars, and most recently, Syrians.

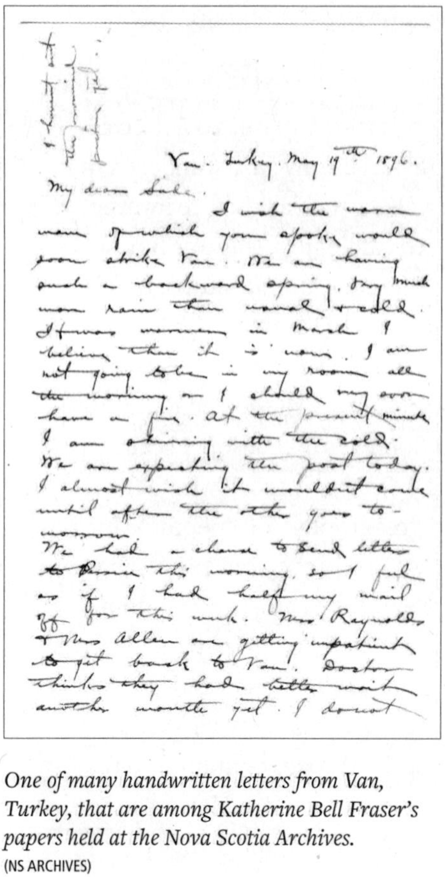

Van. Turkey. May 19th 1896.

My dear Sade.

I wish the warm wave of which you spoke would soon strike Van. We are having such a backward spring. Very much more rain than usual & cold. It was warmer in March I believe than it is now. I am not going to be in my room all the morning or I should [illegible] have a fire. At the present minute I am shivering with the cold. We are expecting the post today. I almost wish it wouldn't come until after the other goes to-morrow. We had a chance to send letters to Russia this morning, so I feel as if I had half my mail off for this week. Mrs. Reynolds & Mrs Allen are getting impatient to get back to Van. Doctor thinks they had better wait another month yet. I donot

One of many handwritten letters from Van, Turkey, that are among Katherine Bell Fraser's papers held at the Nova Scotia Archives.
(NS ARCHIVES)

Katherine Bell Fraser was one of the first of many Canadians who have elected to take the risk of going to a political hotspot to offer aid to those living where religion and/or political affiliation are considered sufficient grounds for persecution and even execution. This young, petite (she was just over five feet tall) nineteenth-century woman from Sherbrooke, Nova Scotia, travelled to Van, Turkey, in 1892 to work at a mission school and hospital helping the minority Armenian Christians. She would also help carry to the world the story of the Armenian massacres, precursors to the Armenian genocide of 1915 when between six hundred thousand and one million Armenian men, women, and children died in local massacres or through mass deportations ordered by the Ottoman government of Turkey. Fearing enemy troops would invade and persuade Armenians to take up arms to overthrow the Ottoman government, which was allied with Germany and Austria-Hungary, the government ordered forced marches that made these Armenians vulnerable to dehydration, disease, starvation, and exposure.

Some might think of global awareness as a twentieth-century invention facilitated by technology and Marshall McLuhan's vision of a "global village." But the story of Katherine Bell Fraser was inspired by something else—something that was very much the product of the time, her community, and her beliefs: Christianity. It was a view both global (in that missionaries wanted to spread "The Good Word" around the world) and limited (in that those who signed up for mission work were predominantly from a world of white privilege—and even in that world, men fared better than women). At times, writing this book was a challenge because the evangelical Christian beliefs of missionaries—reflected in the comment of an American correspondent with the *Christian Herald* about "the Moslem beast"—are far from my own. Reading

The only known portrait of Katherine Bell Fraser in existence.
(NS ARCHIVES)

them, I realized that we are currently seeing these same nineteenth-century sentiments in the news and on social media.

While the desire to spread Christianity might have been the primary and most acceptable reason for a genteel young woman to go to places so foreign, it certainly wasn't the only one. Here in the twenty-first century, international travel is common for twenty-five-year-olds seeking adventure, culture, history, and expanded life experience. Some are moved to work in foreign countries to gain an understanding of other cultures, or to help in humanitarian crises. Katherine Bell Fraser's reasons for going to Turkey in 1892 weren't much different. But she and women like her in the nineteenth century were still in the minority. Women's suffrage was in its infancy. The options for international travel by women were limited and required the oversight and protection of men. Even so, the allure of foreign experiences in the company of other women enticed young Katherine Bell Fraser from the safety of a life in rural Nova Scotia, and even to give up a career as an assistant telegraph operator. She eagerly put them both aside to move halfway around the world to live in a place on the brink of massacres that set the stage, twenty years later, for genocide.

Today, our radios, televisions, and social media burst with stories of war, famine, and humanitarian crises around the globe. We are familiar with work of international aid agencies like the Red Cross and Red Crescent, UNICEF, and Oxfam whose volunteers risk their lives to bring relief to those living in the most horrific circumstances imaginable. Humanitarian agencies such as Amnesty International monitor human rights violations. Médecins sans Frontières supplies medical teams and hospitals to provide medical care in atrocious circumstances.

But such agencies did not exist in the nineteenth century. Missionaries mixed medical aid and education with (usually

Protestant) Christianity and the belief that West was best. The International Committee of the Red Cross, established in Geneva in 1864, addressed medical services on the battlefield. That organization's work in humanitarian relief lay some years in the future. At the time Katherine Bell Fraser and her colleagues sailed from New York in 1892, the American Red Cross's focus was still very much on helping people at home. In 1891, just the year before Fraser arrived in Turkey, the Red Cross in Iowa organized a corn drive for famine relief in Russia. By the time that organization came to the aid of Armenians living in Turkey in the spring of 1896, Fraser and her colleagues had been there almost four years. And they remained a while longer after violence and strict government controls on movement forced the Red Cross to flee Turkey in the summer of 1896.

In the abstract for an article he wrote in 2009, Selim Deringil, an Ottawa-born scholar and professor of history at Lebanese American University, observed: "Although important research has been done about the mass conversions during the [Armenian] genocide of 1915, surprisingly little has focused on the massacres of 1894–1897." Katherine Bell Fraser was a witness to those massacres and the general living conditions endured by Armenians in this period. Her story sheds important light on the efforts by missionaries—many of them women—to provide relief and to save lives. They took great risks to get stories of what was happening to the Armenians to the world, when foreign correspondents were often denied entry to the country or were severely restricted in their movements. Even after the wives and children of US and UK personnel were evacuated from the city of Van in January 1896, Fraser and her female colleagues refused to leave their posts as long as the men remained at theirs, asserting that their work to care for the sick and wounded, and to provide relief to survivors, was as important as any responsibilities of their male colleagues.

"We have lived through dark weeks this fall and winter, and I think we ought to be willing to have worse experiences if necessary," Fraser wrote in her journal. The women remained until they left Van with their male colleagues in August 1896. Even then, Fraser's work was not yet at an end.

Chapter One

"It's rather fun having difficulties to cope with"

Nestled in between St. Marys River and Sherbrooke Lake on Nova Scotia's Eastern Shore lies the village of Sherbrooke. With its small main street, the bucolic setting hosts hundreds of visitors every year to the Nova Scotia Museum's historic Sherbrooke Village site, eager to glimpse what life was like there in the latter part of the nineteenth century. Most are completely unaware of the remarkable woman commemorated by a small monument lying in a cemetery less than a kilometre away from the historic site's entrance gates. Hopefully this book will change that.

Heading along Marine Drive (Nova Scotia Trunk Highway 7) away from the Village, the road passes by the small Riverside Cemetery on the left. Headstones stand in silent remembrance, many of the inscriptions almost obscured by moss and lichen, indicating that those interred are long forgotten. A stone standing to the right of the driveway, a couple of rows up the

Katherine Bell Fraser's headstone reads,
"Doing a man's work with more than a man's capability."
(AUTHOR PHOTO)

hillside, marks the grave of a woman and carries this epitaph: "Doing a man's work with more than a man's capability."

There is no indication that the author was a British consul to Bulgaria in the 1890s, nor why he was moved to pay tribute in this way to the relief efforts of this woman in Turkey and Bulgaria. Time, like the river flowing past the cemetery, has carried on for more than a hundred years since she was laid to rest here.

In stark contrast to the quiet of the cemetery, Sherbrooke in the latter half of the nineteenth century was a bustling community. The discovery of gold in several places along the river in 1861 turned the area almost overnight into a boom town. Hundreds of prospectors from across Canada and the United States, and even a few from overseas, descended on the little Guysborough County community, looking to stake a claim and strike it rich. By 1863, mines had opened in other areas of Nova Scotia, but those at Goldenville near Sherbrooke boasted the highest production. Even so, methods employed at the time helped to remove only a fraction of the gold, and today mining companies are making controversial bids to extract what remains. In the latter half of the nineteenth century, gold fever helped to make Sherbrooke's fortune. Tall ships, salmon, and lumber added diversity—and customers—to the local economy, boosting the bottom lines of local businesses. According to the Sherbrooke Village website, "Funds were found to build or complete the manse, Jail and Court House. In 1864 the Masonic Lodge was formed and by 1868 it was necessary to increase the size of the school."

Prospectors and alcohol were synonymous, but Sherbrooke was a strong temperance community. The Court of Sessions quickly passed a law forbidding the sale of alcohol within the village. That didn't stop groups of "fishermen and Highlanders"

Excelsior (late Chicago) Mill, Goldenville, 1871, by Frederick B. Nichols.
(COURTESY ART GALLERY OF NOVA SCOTIA)

just outside the town limits from making, purchasing, and imbibing alcohol. The website quotes elders of the churches, who urged harsher penalties for public intoxication so that "Sobriety and Temperance which we value more than gold might be preserved." In the end, however, economic prosperity won out and no further penalties were implemented.

Katherine Bell Fraser ("Kathryn," "Katie," or "KBF" as she most frequently signed her letters and is henceforth known in this book) was born in this prosperous community on June 5, 1867, the youngest of six children born to John Fraser and Mary Jane McDonald. Sherbrooke was, at the time of her birth, just starting to enjoy its new prosperity with the discovery of gold only six years earlier. Her father was a lumberman, working to take wood from Guysborough forests to Sherbrooke mills. He provided comfortably for his family, ensuring that sons and daughters alike received a good education and a solid foundation in the Presbyterian Church. The eldest child, William

Frederick (known as Fred), followed his father's example and became a lumberman, though eventually he would be drawn to Arizona, where he died in 1900, aged forty-three. Their other son, Daniel McDonald Fraser, became a miner. The daughters—Christina (Tina), Edith, Ella, and Katherine—learned the domestic arts and household management in preparation for making good marriage matches.

There are scant records of KBF's early life. Her mother died when she was seventeen. Two years later, KBF moved to Yarmouth, Nova Scotia, to take a position as an assistant telegraph operator in the Western Union Telegraph Office there, sending messages around the world at the rate of twenty-five cents per word.

There is a five-year gap between KBF's arrival in Yarmouth in 1887 and her departure for Turkey in 1892 that is not covered by her journal or correspondence yet found or, possibly, still in existence. Presumably she enjoyed her job and became involved in the local church and community. Daily steamships or trains between Yarmouth and Halifax with connections to Sherbrooke made possible trips home to see family. Mail coaches carried the mail daily via Halifax, providing KBF with the means to keep up with family news and to keep them apprised of events in her life.

Many people in southwest Nova Scotia had ties to "the Boston States," and the sea was an important route carrying goods and people between Nova Scotia and Boston. Passenger steamships, *Yarmouth* and *Boston*, ran four times per week between the two ports for which they were named. Travellers could also opt to take the train to Halifax and catch one of the steamships that travelled to Boston daily from that city.

KBF's cousin Sadie married a Princeton professor of Classics. KBF made several visits to see her cousin in New

Jersey and enjoy the culture Princeton had to offer. During one visit, KBF heard a physician, Grace Kimball, speak about the plight of Christian Armenians living under Turkish Ottoman rule. Kimball was passionate about her humanitarian work, which was rooted in and inextricably linked to her deep and abiding Christian faith, with a bias against Muslims not unusual for its time (nor, for some, in ours). In an address made to a meeting of the Women's Board of Foreign Missions in Boston in 1897, Kimball said:

> In Turkey we have existing side by side two races and two religions, the Turks and the Armenians, Mohammedanism and Christianity. The Turks have the greater power, in numbers and authority. But Mohammedanism has outlived whatever usefulness it may have once had. It is a dying and retrogressive religion, and inevitably places its followers in opposition to progress. A dying religion is always a fanatical religion. The more the Turks feel (and they do feel it keenly) that their power is passing away, the more fanatical they become.
>
> On the other hand, here are the Armenians, numbering in Turkey two million at the utmost, and scattered all over the Empire; a race with a religion antagonistic to Mohammedanism, and with an independent church, neither Greek nor Roman, but Gregorian, a church with a glorious history, which is very dear to them; a race full of enterprise and the spirit of advancement, much like ourselves in characteristics, and full of possibilities of every kind. Here we have existing side by side the retrogressive Turkish majority, and this small but plucky, independent and enterprising race, who are the

bankers, merchants, artisans and laborers of Turkey. It is impossible that conflict should not arise. Each race and religion looks upon the other as unclean, and this antagonism runs through all the relations of life.

At the end of the nineteenth century, the city of Van was in the province of Armenia, Turkey, on the eastern edge of the Ottoman Empire, just over a hundred kilometres from the borders of Russia to the northeast and Persia (what is now Iran) to the east. Here, Armenian Christians lived in relative peace with their Muslim neighbours, whom they outnumbered by about three to one. Most Armenians—many of them merchants and artisans—lived in the section of Van called Aikesdan, "The Garden City," where homes and villas had orchards and lush gardens of flowers and vegetables. It was here that New Hampshire–born Vassar graduate Grace Kimball first arrived in 1882 to work as a missionary on behalf of the Congregational Church's American Board of Commissions for Foreign Missions (referred to by KBF in her correspondence as "the American Board" or simply "the Board") at the Girls' Boarding and Day school there. Kimball quickly realized that people in Van—particularly women and children—were in greater need of doctors

KBF was inspired by Dr. Grace Kimball, who spoke at Princeton about the plight of Christian Armenians living under Turkish Ottoman rule. (COURTESY THE POUGHKEEPSIE PUBLIC LIBRARY DISTRICT)

than missionaries. Six years later, she returned to the US to study medicine at the Woman's Medical College in New York City. After graduating in 1892, she returned to Turkey to practice medicine, accompanied by a group of women to assist her in the mission hospital and to teach at the mission school, among them Katherine Bell Fraser. Kimball's experiences and eyewitness accounts in the 1890s were key to scholars and historians in tracking the lead-up to the subsequent Armenian genocide of 1915.

Though Kimball's words about Muslims are shocking to some and still echoed by others in the twenty-first century, they were commonly held at a time when imperialism wasn't questioned and colonialism forced change on those who were considered inferior if they weren't white and Christian. As a young, Christian woman of her times, unaware of her own ignorance—of Islam, of "Gregorian" Christianity, and of the ancient cultures and traditions of both Turks and Armenians—KBF heard Kimball "speechify" in this manner and felt eager to go to Turkey to help those poor unfortunates "much like ourselves in characteristics." Fraser grew up in colonial Nova Scotia and, as such, saw those who were not British or American as at best novel and curious, and at worst, barbaric—Muslim and Gregorian Christian alike. While accepting that some people were less than others, she believed that education (which often took the form of indoctrination) could elevate them. She could not know what it was to be of a people who were looked upon by their rulers as dispensable—not worthy of life, except perhaps as slaves—but she understood the injustice of it.

At the same time, however, her letters home described the Armenians oppressed in Ottoman Turkey as not only different, but inferior: "His wife is a very beautiful woman, has a perfect Madonna face and for an Armenian, is very intelligent"; "She was not at all like the usual Armenian, but refined and gentle in her manner"; "Aghavne is a very sweet little girl, more like a white person—wouldn't that make the Armenians mad—than any of the others."

KBF's beliefs came from the class system of the time, making distinctions between one type of Christian and another (e.g., Protestant vs. Catholic), and non-white and white Christians. When considered as a whole, however, Christians—regardless of type and colour—required defence against "infidels" (a term used not only by Muslims to describe Christians, but also by Christians to describe Muslims).

However, Fraser did not paint the Turks and Kurds (people from the neighbouring province of Kurdistan with Persian origins and an Arabic language separate from Turkish) as complete villains, either. And interestingly, given her devout Christian faith, which clearly delineated "right" from "wrong," she observed the Muslim custom of a man having many wives as curious rather than sinful, and expressed no aversion to taking afternoon tea with the harem of the local vali (governor). On at least one occasion, toward the end of her stay in Armenia, she was the overnight guest of a harem.

The distaste and occasional disdain Fraser expresses in her early letters concerning those whom she had travelled over half a world to help, is initially surprising. If she had so little regard for them, what possessed her to travel so far, risk exposure to serious diseases, live in conditions both inferior and foreign to those back home, and ultimately to stay well beyond the time to which she initially committed herself?

One possibility is that she saw it as her Christian duty. In a letter to her sisters shortly after she arrived in Constantinople she said that her decision to undertake the trip "seemed right," though she didn't elaborate whether this feeling was spiritual or personal. Another is that, as the youngest and unmarried daughter of the family, she did not want to have to assume the duties of caring for the family's widowed and aging patriarch. In several letters to her sister Tina, also still single at the time and six years KBF's senior, KBF apologizes for not being close to home to help out with filial duties, but the fact that these regrets are dashed off in a few words leads the reader to question whether she is sincerely sorry or simply grateful to have dodged that bullet.

It's also possible that the spirit of adventure and idealism with which she started changed with time and first-hand experience to a deeper understanding of those with whom she worked. Point form notes pencilled in small script in the back of her journal are verbs and nouns stripped of adjectives, recording the brutality and inhumanity she witnessed. They are the bare bones of memory that will be developed in articles published in American newspapers toward the end of her tenure in Turkey, when everything looks hopelessly "black, black...."

Missionary staff were well aware that letters might be intercepted and read by Turkish government officials. By describing everything she witnessed in her letters, KBF not only risked alarming her family, but also risked compromising the very work in which she and her colleagues were engaged. Maintaining, or at least appearing to maintain neutrality was key if the Turkish government was to permit them to remain, so initially she confined details of what she learned and witnessed to the pages of her journal, while writing in letters what she believed Turkish officials would want her to report to her family. Eventually, however, she cast aside this caution with the increasing possibility that she would die in the massacres, deciding to publish regardless of whether she perished.

Fraser's early letters home give the impression to Turkish authorities who opened and read at random the letters of foreigners living in Turkey, that she had no great concern for the Armenians, even while working amongst them as a teacher. Hence, descriptions in her letters home of Armenian garb or customs as "barbaric" and her dismissive comment of one woman as being intelligent "for an Armenian." These comments do not appear in her journal. If written in letters intercepted by the authorities, however, comments such as these might remove her from any suspicion of sympathy for the more radical, revolutionary activities of some of the young people with whom she came in contact.

The articles that KBF mailed home or carried into Persia for publication in America in late 1895 tell a very different story than her early letters home. They speak of slaughter, of hunger, of unspeakable inhumanity. Initially, in both her letters home and her personal journal, Fraser is incredulous that such things could really be happening. Then she finds that they are but cannot let herself believe they're happening on the scale claimed by the Armenians. And when she finds out that that, too, is true, she is conflicted. She feels the Revolutionists (Armenian socialists) are unnecessarily putting people's lives at risk. Regardless, she commits to helping those who depend on her—her students—and to lending her voice to the growing chorus telling the world what is happening to the Armenians at the hands of the Turkish government. In her final months in Armenia, after hundreds are killed and atrocities are committed, she confesses that, if she'd had to endure such suffering and brutality, she would have been driven to rebellion, too.

KBF's letters home begin aboard the SS *Werra*, steaming out of New York midday on a hot, sticky July 28, 1892. There is neither record nor discussion of her preparations, whether she returned home to Sherbrooke to bid goodbye to her family before heading to Turkey via Europe. Regardless, she knew her sisters had reservations about her decision. And she knew that her father and brothers were not in favour of her trip, not necessarily because she was a woman, but because she had no clear idea what she was letting herself in for. Then again, neither did they. Their only information came from newspapers and pamphlets. At that point, there was little indication of what was to come over the next few years.

This biography of one woman must be set within the context of her time. Given the complexities of politics, however, it is a challenge to give that context without appearing to oversimplify or overlook key factors. There are many excellent books about the circumstances leading up to the Armenian genocide in 1915, the genocide itself, and the aftermath. Those wishing for more detail might be interested in Taner Akçam's *A Shameful Act* (2006) or Peter Balakian's *The Burning Tigris* (2004). For the purposes of KBF's story, a brief summary of the situation in Turkey in the 1890s provides some context and sheds light on why she volunteered to go there.

"The Armenian Question," as it came to be known, first came to international attention following the Russo-Ottoman War of 1877–78. But the oppression of Armenians under Ottoman rule had deeper roots. An inequitable tax system, looting and murder by Kurds that was ignored by police and government officials, a judicial system that did not permit Armenian testimony (unless it favoured the government), and ineligibility for military service or to own arms were just a few of the grievances experienced over twenty years and cited in a report the Armenian Communal Council submitted to the Ottoman government in March 1872.

The Ottoman government responded by setting up a commission composed equally of Muslims and non-Muslims to investigate the allegations. But the revolt by the Christian minority against the Ottoman Empire in Bosnia-Herzegovina in 1875, followed by uprisings in Bulgaria and Serbia, changed everything. The bloody and brutal suppression of these protests by the Ottoman Empire caused an international outcry. European leaders threatened action, citing the 1856 Treaty of Paris as giving them the right to protect the Christian minority under the Sultan's rule. Accordingly, Great Britain and Russia came together in 1877 (shortly before the Russo-Turkish War) to establish the London Protocol, the ninth article of which granted the Great Powers (Austria-Hungary, France, Germany, Great Britain and Ireland, Italy, Russia) the authority to undertake joint action against the Ottoman Empire if it objected to the proposed reforms for the Christian minority. One wonders what part of their actions were from genuine concern for the rights of minority Christians and what part stemmed from commercial interests in the area. Not surprisingly, the Ottoman Empire did object. But when the Treaty of Berlin was drawn up in 1878 at the end of the Russo-Turkish War, the Ottoman Empire lost its major holdings in Europe. The ninth article of the London Protocol became the sixty-first article of the Treaty of Berlin, forcing the Ottoman Empire to accept that the Great Powers would monitor the Christian minority living under Turkish rule, to ensure their rights were upheld.

Although the United States was not a signatory to the Treaty of Berlin, its missionaries had a long history of working in the Near East. Their presence in the Ottoman Empire was established in 1819, initially in the hope of converting Muslims to Christianity. After coming to the conclusion they were fighting an uphill and losing battle, they turned their attention to the Ottoman Empire's Christian minority, whose Apostolic Christianity—with deeper roots and a longer history than the evangelical and Presbyterian denominations on which the missions were based—the missionaries considered nominal to their own. In a 2009 article, Ann Marie Wilson noted: "With over four million dollars in property holdings, the American missionary presence was far greater than that of any other European power; it also overshadowed the importance of US business interests in the region. Consequently, American consuls in the Ottoman Empire directed much of their energy toward protecting the safety and legal rights of missionaries and their families."

Three Armenian political parties formed during the five-year period between 1885 and 1890. The first was the Armenakan Party (or Armenists, as KBF refers to them) in Van, a secret society whose meetings took place literally underground, in an area used to press grapes. Members supported Armenian self-rule and self-defence against violence. The second was the Hunchak Party, formed in Geneva by Russian Armenians with strong Marxist leanings. The third was the Dashnaktsutyun, or Armenian Revolutionary Federation, known simply as "Revolutionists." Though ostensibly all worked for the freedom of Armenians, there was some resentment among Armenians living in Turkey about the Armenians coming to fight from outside the country. In the beginning, KBF thought Hunchak and Revolutionists were only troublemakers.

Though its actions toward its Christian minority were atrocious and brutal, the Ottoman Empire was a political entity that deemed itself to have the same right to self governance as did the members of the Great Powers, even if it included religious and political oppression of minorities under its rule. The United States had only just abolished slavery in

1865 without a similar threat of foreign intervention, though, granted, the action came from within in the form of a civil war. This may seem somewhat of an "apples and oranges" comparison. The Ottoman Empire was a Muslim majority state in which minority Christians lived. The United States was a Christian country in which lived people of African descent—most of them Christian at that time—and in which Christians themselves (in particular Baptists, Methodists, Presbyterians) were divided along north/south lines when it came to the question of slavery.

The humanitarian crisis to which KBF and her colleagues responded in 1892 was the result of the actions of Sultan Abdul Hamid II. The following account appeared in an article written by Rev. Cyrus Hamlin entitled "The Armenian Massacres," published in *The Outlook* in December 1895. It is certainly not an unbiased account. But it provides a contemporary Christian view and some insight into why people like KBF were inspired to go to Turkey to help with the cause.

> Turkey has no invariable policy which controls successive Sultans. Mahmoud II was a great reformer. He destroyed the Janizaries [elite infantry units of which the Sultan's bodyguards were members], reorganized the army, relieved the "rayahs" [members of the tax-paying lower class] (Christians and Jews) of many burdens and humiliations, and aimed to establish friendly relations with the European States, and to have a regular cabinet of ministers. The rayahs regarded him as their friend. The fanatical Moslems called him a giaour [infidel]. He employed many Armenians in the under offices of state. One was his chief architect, one the collector of customs, another the head of the mint;

and he made an American, Mr. Eckford, the chief of the naval arsenal. Under his reign the Turks had to respect the rights of Christians.

He had a reign of just thirty-one years, full of incidents, and weakened by a disastrous war with Russia and the rebellion of Mehmet Ali, the Pasha of Egypt.

His son, Abdul Medjid, came to the throne in 1839—a boy of sixteen. He endeavored to push forward his father's design to Europeanize the government. He issued the celebrated constitution called the "Hatti-Scheriff of Gulhane." He introduced many Armenians into government employ. The old Turkish party, the unchangeable Moslem, was disgusted with his reforms, as was Russia. A reaction became dominant in 1843, and the old party again ruled, to the terror of the rayahs. But the great English ambassador, Sir Stratford Canning, took the Sultan under his protection, and many important improvements were made in the administration, and generally in favor of equal rights to the Christian subjects.

The Crimean War saved Constantinople from the grasp of Russia, but the peace of Paris, through the treason and ambition of Louis Napoleon, rejected the policy of England and gave Turkey over entirely to herself, forbidding all interference from any one of the signatory powers. From that time onward the condition of the rayahs can hardly be said to have improved. Abdul Medjid died after a reign of twenty-two years—'39 to '61. Abdul Aziz, the successor, was stupid and brutal. He got the finances into hopeless entanglements by excessive loans at ruinous interest,

> and by palace squanderings. Russia made him her tool for the ruin of the Empire. June 4, 1876, he was found dead in his chamber, having been assassinated or having committed suicide. There were two parties to that question, but all agree that he died, and his memory may as well perish.
>
> We now come to the present reigning Sultan, Abdul Hamid. He has always been regarded as a fanatical Mussulman. He came to the throne with the inborn resolution to exercise all the power of the successor of the Prophet. He is a skilful diplomat. He believes in the supreme power of lying. He covers up all that he does by falsehood or false testimony. He can always bring any number of witnesses to prove that there has been no violence where hundreds have been slaughtered.

The author's linking of the ability to be a "skilful diplomat" with "the supreme power of lying" is worth noting, used in a pejorative sense when referring to a "Mussulman." Hamlin's contemporary account does not differ greatly from modern representations of Abdul Hamid II as not just fanatical, but a dangerously paranoid ruler who hated the Christian minority in his country and showed little regard for his fellow Muslims. A number of Turkish intellectuals and journalists (among them British Prime Minister Boris Johnson's great-grandfather, Ali Kemal) were banished from the country. Abdul Hamid II's fear that his own military would overthrow him led him eventually to stop paying their salaries and to venture forth rarely from the fortified residence he built for himself and his family in Constantinople.

As stories of the situation in Armenia reached Boston and New York, a number of people who took up the cause for the abolition of slavery and for women's suffrage also involved themselves in "the Armenian Question." The abolitionist William Lloyd Garrison Jr.; Republican Party founder Henry Blackwell; poet Alice Stone Blackwell; abolitionist and activist Julia Ward Howe (author of "The Battle Hymn of the Republic" and a distant cousin of Nova Scotia journalist and political reformer Joseph Howe); and the Reverend Samuel June Barrows, publisher of the *Christian Register*, all lent their voices to the cause. The *Christian Register* would provide significant funds to the Van mission and the work of Grace Kimball and her colleagues.

KBF didn't call herself a "feminist" or even a supporter of women's suffrage in any of her letters or her journal. But the fact that Elizabeth Stuart Phelps—who challenged traditional male and female roles in marriage and family, and anticipated the bra-burnings of the 1970s when, in 1874, she urged women to burn their corsets—was one of her favourite authors, provides a possible clue about where her sympathies lay. The fact remains that at twenty-two KBF was earning her own living away from home and travelling independently between Nova Scotia and Princeton, where she attended lectures given by people like Grace Kimball. And at the age of twenty-five, KBF felt perfectly capable of making the decision to live and work in Turkey regardless of her family's opinions and wishes.

There is nothing in KBF's papers describing her first meeting with Grace Kimball or her reasons for enlisting and accepting paid passage, room, and a modest stipend for her services. Perhaps it was a combination of the call to adventure and a Christian zeal to help the unfortunate. In some of the literature of the time there is a professed desire to convert Muslims to Christianity. But with the realization of the enormity and fruitlessness of such a task, evangelical Christians satisfied themselves with the prospect of converting Nestorian and Gregorian (Armenian Orthodox and Armenian Catholic) Christians to Protestantism, all the while providing relief for the poor, the downtrodden, and the oppressed.

Fraser's experiences gave meaning and colour to her life, while frequently enraging her and trying her patience. Years later, she would write of the ups and downs of her work: "It's rather fun having difficulties to cope with. And always I shall try to keep very near to the 'Source of all Good.' 'Inshallah' it is so."

Chapter Two

"I was completely carried away"

The novelty of the initial part of KBF's transatlantic journey in the company of nine other women—two female physicians (Dr. Kimball and Dr. Smith, whom KBF sometimes refers to as "Miss Smith"), a missionary's wife and her two nieces, and four mission school teachers like herself—is evident in the first letters she wrote to her sisters. The voyage was not without incident. Before reaching Gibraltar, seasickness rendered at least part of the passage unpleasant (KBF pointed out that, though feeling unwell or "rather shaky" at times, she never became seasick), and three passengers died: a twenty-two-year-old man, and a mother and child. All were buried at sea at midnight, after passengers had retired for the night. Any still up and about were not permitted to attend the service.

The group's projected arrival at Van, Turkey, was sometime in late September. Until then, KBF looked forward to "quite a little bit of visiting," with stops in Gibraltar, Genoa, Milan, and Venice—where she hoped some letters from home awaited her at the Hotel Aurora—and on to Trieste (still part of Austria at that time), Patras, and Athens. The timing of their voyage across to Constantinople and the overland journey to Van was dependent on whether outbreaks of cholera would require quarantine.

But neither the possible inconveniences of the journey, nor the perils of labours that lay in the future were in mind when she wrote her sisters of approaching Gibraltar on the first of August.

> The entrance to the Strait is magnificent, Spanish coast to one side & the African on the other. You cannot imagine how excited we became when they told us land was in sight. We rushed first to one side of the ship & then to the other, not to miss seeing Africa as well as Spain. Immense hills seemed to rise straight out of the water, but after a little a mist settled on the African side & we gave our full attention to Gibraltar side. The land did not rise as abruptly & there were several villages down by the shore which looked very quiet & peaceful in the early morning. In the distance the mountains seemed very high & bare looking.
>
> I was busily studying one of the hills when some one exclaimed there's Gibraltar! & I turned to behold the grandest sight I ever saw. It is much higher & bolder looking than in the photographs altho' I think the one I bought on shore is very good. You'll see it some day. It did not take very long for us to run into the Bay & after lunch we went ashore. Almost before our anchor was down boats shot out from the shore with fruit of all kinds & fancy wares, handkerchiefs silk scarves fans

> etc., such a babel of sounds. It was splendid fun getting off the ship & ashore in a sail boat. Some went in row boats, others on the steam launch & some poor souls did not get off at all. The Capt said he would sail at 1.30 which gave us a short hour ashore. He said it would not be safe to go as he would not wait a minute. Most of us risked it, stayed nearly two hours & got back & were rec'd smilingly by the Capt. who said "You didn't get left after all."

There followed descriptions of donkey- or horse-drawn carriages that took them along narrow streets, past "picturesque looking children & ladies; the latter wore those black silk drapes on their heads as only the Spanish beauties know how to wear them." She noted that the "Moorish costume was pretty, saw several men in that garb, long crimson cloak which blew back & showed baggy trousers to the knee, bare legs below & a fancy sandle [*sic*] on foot. They wore gayly coloured scarves around waist."

As a territory of Great Britain bordering Spain, Gibraltar was a "web of fortifications" housing "6000 soldiers...350 cannon...and, I think they said, always enough food to last 20 years." On the streets of the city nestled at the bottom of the famous rock, they saw "lots of English soldiers, Scotch Highlanders & people we see every day." Presumably those who reminded this young Nova Scotian woman of "people we see every day" were white Europeans.

KBF delighted in the novelty of buildings of "grayish" stone and those of "pretty cream" or "dazzling white" and wrote, "Along one street there was an exceedingly beautiful hedge of aloes surrounded by pink Oleanders. Right alongside there was a hedge of heliotrope & inside such cool & shady trees which I should think would be highly prized in a place where it is so hot & so few cool spots to rest."

Her descriptions of Genoa and of going on a "tramp" with a local guide whom she describes as "such fun" and "good natured" evokes the 1985 Merchant/Ivory film based on E. M. Forster's book *A Room with a View* (though that story was set largely in Florence). We get a sense of her slight discomfort at being in a foreign place while at the same time being thoroughly captivated by the local sights and colour. About the twelfth-century Cathedral San Lorenzo, she writes:

> It has been changed some since then, part looks quite modern. It is black & white marble alternate courses. The inside was draped for today (a holy day of some kind) in red & the altars were trimmed with flowers. I was in again this A.M. when all the candles were lighted & the light was very fine. The music was perfect. The organ has a very rich tone & the vocal music was excellent. They have John Baptist buried in the church, remains brought from Palestine. No ladies allowed entrance to the chapel where he is kept because t'was one who had him beheaded. Suppose we shall find his precious dust in several other churches before a week is over....

WHILE SHE COULD APPRECIATE THE AESTHETIC VALUE OF THE church, her comment about John the Baptist's head is borne of her upbringing in a no-nonsense Protestant denomination with less inclination for the bells-and-smells, saints-and-relics of the Roman church. Of a visit to the Campo Santo cemetery, she wrote that while some of the tombs of wealthy people were "beautifully done and the decorations appropriate...[o]thers were perfectly ludicrous."

One evening, KBF and five of the young women in her travelling group expressed a desire to go to the exposition grounds to witness events being staged there. Dr. H. N. Barnum, an American missionary based in Harput (an ancient village in eastern Turkey) and their chaperone, declared that he was too tired to accompany them. Their disappointment quickly turned to excitement when a Mr. Jewett, an American consul staying in the hotel and on his way home from Turkey, offered to escort them. Because he was a friend of Mr. Barnum's, the invitation was accepted readily.

Though KBF doesn't say what the exposition was about, she describes their excitement about having to take several carriages because there were so many of them, and Mr. Jewett's efforts to keep them all together: "Every few minutes Mr. J. would count us off 1, 2, 3, 4, 5, 6 all right—come along." After a cursory glance at the exhibits (for KBF provided no description in her journal or letters), they headed out to "the Landing where the music and the people were."

Her description suggests that it was a *son et lumière* featuring "such charming music too & such a gay throng. I enjoyed seeing the people almost as much as anything. I like the faces of the better class of Italians. They are different from what I expected to see. The grounds were like a scene in fairyland, a large fountain in the centre kept continually changing from one colour to another then all the colours at once & shaded from dainty shades to the very deep ones." She goes into no detail about the faces of "the better class of Italians" or how they differed from others; she assumes her sisters will know. The evening concluded with a parade of red, blue, and green lights carried by students on large poles, with the size of the lights increasing with the procession, until she marvelled how anyone could carry such a large glass globe hoisted on a single pole.

During her time in Genoa, KBF took several treks around the city along its narrow streets, some "paved with wood" and others in "round stones." She marvelled, "It is a very hilly city & has many splendid villas & palaces, built away up so high it almost makes one dizzy to look up." She travelled to Pegli, a suburb of Genoa, to the Villa Pallavicini, which featured a park in the English romantic style. Though easily accessible from modern-day Genoa, the journey was not as easy for KBF's group. Even so, she wrote that the villa and grounds

> well repaid us for our very long drive.... At the very top there was an old Roman tower, rather an imitation one from the top of which there is a magnificent view of the sea, hills & Genoa in the distance. There are Greek temples, Chinese & Turkish kiosks, a Cleopatra's needle, stalacktite [*sic*] grotto into which we went & discovered water, with two row boats ready waiting. We got in & were rowed out into the open air—there is a very pretty view from the outset. The park was charming I assure you & well worth spending two or three hours in. Miss Kimball took her Kodak along & used it on several occasions, although the guide insisted it was against the rules.

From their next stop, Milan, KBF wrote her sisters that, although she was enjoying the trip, she "[h]ad a small fit of home sickness one evening but I am not going to allow myself the indulgence very often." The feeling might have been induced by the trip from Genoa, which they left at nine in the morning, to Milan. Though the journey was pleasant enough to begin with, "through fertile valleys surrounded by beautiful hills," the route passed through "twenty-four tunnels...the longest was five miles, another, two" with only one rest stop. They arrived in Milan at two thirty in the afternoon, "a very soiled & begrimed looking crowd when we arrived at Hotel Pozzo."

Despite the inauspicious introduction, she found Milan

> more modern than Genoa & and entirely different but a lovely city. The streets are wide & the walks have shading trees on each side, which make them cool & pleasant. One street had two immense rows on each side of horse chestnuts. They were lovely & shaded even the middle of the wide street. The public gardens are beautiful & the cemetery too is a pretty spot. There is a small building after the style of the Campo Santo in Genoa, but not nearly as fine & of course fewer monuments. We drove through the older part of the town. The streets are much narrower & more irregular, but comparatively clean. The shops are very nice & goods cheap, altho' they sometimes ask pretty big prices in the beginning. It's very funny how they come down if they think one is not going to take the article. I like a fixed price better, of course, a reasonable one. Yesterday I bought a pair of coloured eyeglasses for 20 cts same as Dr. Kimball paid $1.50 for in America. 20 cts was first price.

She describes a visit to "the chapel" for Sunday service, where she "didn't enjoy the sermon in Italian altho' the priest was very demonstrative in the delivery." Her subsequent description of a place so "perfectly grand...[i]ts immensity takes one's breath away and keeps one very quiet for at least a few minutes" is hardly that of a chapel but of a cathedral. Nowhere does she mention its name. She finds one of the many statues, with its flayed skin "hung over its shoulders... perfectly awful." She believes it to be St. Ambrose, so it's possible that she was in the Basilica of Sant'Ambrogio, but as St. Ambrose was not flayed alive, the statue depicting a flayed man would most likely have been that of St. Bartholemew in the Duomo di Milano. (Bartholemew, one of the twelve apostles, was martyred in Armenia when he was flayed and beheaded. He and another apostle, Jude Thaddeus, are credited with bringing Christianity to Armenia and are the patron saints of the Armenian Apostolic Church.)

KBF's amazement at her first sight of flying buttresses, which she described to her sisters as "half arches...beautifully carved," and her descriptions of the statues, the pillars, and the decoration of "the chapel" are further evidence that she was most likely in the Duomo di Milano, the largest cathedral in Italy and the fifth largest in the world, renowned for all the features she describes. With Dr. Kimball she ascends 494 steps in a tower rising 65 metres, from the top of which they see panoramic views of the city below and the mist-covered hills around. KBF could not summon words to describe what lay before her. There was nothing in Nova Scotia, Princeton, or Boston to which she could compare it for her sisters.

Dr. Barnum and his wife departed from Milan on August 8 with four of the mission teachers, bound for Constantinople. That left Drs. Kimball and Smith with KBF and two other mission teachers, identified only as Miss Hamblin and Miss Yale, to continue their European tour.

At their next stop, Verona, KBF writes enthusiastically of her visit to the Certosa di Pavia, a Carthusian monastery commissioned by hereditary lord and first Duke of Milan, Gian Galeazzo Visconti. (Although she mentions a fresco featuring the image of "Galeazzino" Visconti, she seems unaware that he is responsible for the monastery's existence.) Once again, she is amazed at the extent of the place, the elaborateness of its decoration, and the beauty of both grounds and building with its "seven chapels either side of the nave." She writes, "in the north transept [is a monument to] one of the Founders." She does not realize this is the tomb of the same "Galeazinno" Visconti to whom she referred earlier.

The effect of the Certosa di Pavia is overwhelming and almost too much for her to try to describe. She says to her sisters, "I've not told you one quarter of it. One forgets unless they write it at once & besides it's impossible to write it all down. But I would not have missed it for a good deal." Though well schooled in Biblical studies, familiar with the classics, and a devotee of Byron, nothing KBF had previously learned or experienced in her twenty-five years prepared her for these experiences. Similarly, though in the opposite extreme, nothing prepared her for what she was to learn and experience in Armenia. Until then, she could revel in the beauty that greeted her in each of her stops in Italy, Austria, Switzerland, and Greece en route to Turkey.

If she thought she could see no more breathtaking scenery to astonish and delight her, she had not anticipated what awaited her on "a circular trip around the lakes," starting with Lake Como. "The scenery was grand. On each side the hills rose in stately piles. They were covered with green to the top & many pretty villas & terraced gardens were scattered along by the water. Every few miles a lovely village or town. The water was so pretty, a lovely shade of rich green & wound in & out among the hills. I was completely carried away."

They spent the night at Cadenabbia where the view from her hotel was "sublime" and where, she confessed, she would be content to remain for "weeks and weeks." Instead, they took a rowboat the next morning to Menaggio, where they caught a train for Lake Lugano on the Italian/Swiss border. “It was quite an engineering feat to run a railway across those mountains & tunnel through solid rock. It seemed to me as if we should surely go back down the hills or fall over into the chasms but we arrived at our destination safely & after a ride through beautiful scenery.”

Back in Milan once more, she wrote her sisters: “Milan Cathedral is grand, the Certossa magnificent but the Lakes & Mountains are sublime. One feels so small & little in the presence of such master work. I think nature builds the best.”

From Milan they went by rail to Verona, where KBF heard “such sweet music coming from the street below” her hotel room that she wondered playfully if it could be “my sweet Romeo serenading me.” They enjoyed the romance of the Capulet home and were intrigued by the ruins of a Roman arena dating from Diocletian’s time, where a guide showed them areas where gladiators once congregated and pens where animals waited until the inevitable and bloody life-and-death matches.

Her first experience of Venice was not nearly as favourable. Arriving at the station at six thirty P.M. and with a one-hour gondola ride to get to their hotel, they were too tired to do anything other than partake of a light supper at the hotel and go straight to bed. To make matters worse, the proprietor of the Hôtel Aurora, where someone recommended they stay, was “a perfect bear of a man.” And if that was an inauspicious beginning, there was more to come. “To bed, but alas in my case, not to sleep...as there was no screen on my bed & the mosquitoes bothered the life nearly out of me.... About 2 o’clock I got up & put on a thick blue veil which kept away the flies but was not conducive to good sleep. You should see my face....

There is not a square inch of it not covered with bites. You would think I had the measles very badly, but I resolve to have a good time & see the city notwithstanding a blotched face."

True to her word, she rallied the following day and "a walk around to St. Mark's Square this morning put me in a better humour & I hope to enjoy our four days stay in the 'City on the Sea.'" In the light of day, and having had at least a few hours' sleep, she was in a better frame of mind to appreciate and even be charmed by her surroundings, starting with the station at which she had arrived the night before:

> Coming out of the station, before us was a broad flight of stone steps at the foot of which there were 25–30 gondolas, black painted boats with high indented iron prows, seats upholstered in black leather with black canopies. The only bit of color in the whole boat is the brass handles or ornaments on each side, to which the cords of the canopy are attached. But the gondoliers wear suits of white with dark blue sailor collars & sashes, or trimmings of red which give them the color required. We were soon gliding over the Grand Canal to our hotel, in a much more comfortable & picturesque conveyance than the cabs of our towns at home. It is perfectly wonderful how they escape colliding with other boats & how they turn corners so closely & not touch. After a charming ride through narrow streets we came out into the canal again passed the Ducal Palace & the Bridge of Sighs (which has a scaffolding around it for repairs therefore is not as interesting looking as it might be) & was soon at our hotel.

She took breakfast on her first full day in Venice at a café in St. Mark's Square consisting "of rolls & fresh butter (I mean without salt, not only new), honey or jam, coffee or chocolate. Nothing else unless specifically ordered. We have enjoyed our early repast very much indeed!"

They were due to spend a few days in Venice before catching a train to Trieste where, after a few days, they would take a steamer to Athens. But while still in Venice, word reached them of an outbreak of cholera in various ports along the Black Sea. If it spread to Constantinople, they faced the prospect of having to spend the winter in that city—and that was a possibility KBF did not welcome. Until now, illness and misfortune were remote possibilities. But as she drew closer to her destination and the realities it held, a hint of fear crept into the tone of her letters. She said to her sisters, "Perhaps you had better not say anything about this to Father as he will worry about it unnecessarily & please do not think too much of it yourself. We will trust I shall be as well taken care of as at home & escape cholera & all other dread diseases & return to you in safety in a few short years."

She describes St. Mark's Square and the facade of the "world famed structure" of St. Mark's Basilica, which she says is "gorgeous and dazzling in the sunlight." She continues, "You feel slightly disappointed on entering but after a while you wonder how man ever could do such work." She concludes that there is much to see and vows to make several visits in order to take it all in. Besides the cathedral, there are galleries and other churches to visit, all of them containing works of great Italian artists. She refers her sisters to John Ruskin's *The Stones of Venice*—a three-volume work published about forty years earlier—for more details of what she has seen.

Not all of their time was spent travelling to one place or another. There was also time to enjoy the local colour.

Before going to dinner last evening we took a gondola & went up through the canal. I never enjoyed a more pleasant hour. The sun was just setting, one mass of crimson & gold. We started from the lagoon, which was a beautiful blue with the yellow sand bars showing through. Several large steamers anchored near, were dressed with bunting & added beauty & many small sail boats, with loads of pleasure seekers sailing about, but when we got into the canal it was glorious. Gondolas with picturesque boatmen & gaily dressed occupants floated by, small steam boats with decks crowded with excursionists kept passing & repassing, odd shaped boats with a merry party of students, another with Armenians, picturesque caps of red & sailor suits, they came from an Armenian college on one of the islands. On each side of us rose the grand facades of the old palaces beautiful in decay. Some few have been restored & as we went slowly along the windows were lighted up & gave us a peep inside of the beautiful homes. One gondola stopped at the door of a lovely home & immediately a female voice began the sweetest song, joined in the chorus by male & female voices. It was very charming. We could not tell whether it was meant for a serenade or not but it added to our enjoyment whether they were pleased or not.

The sun set was the loveliest of all. I never saw more gorgeous coloring. The sky was such a dainty pale blue, then a pink as faint in color, shading into the richest crimson & when the sun had set it turned into burning gold. No wonder Italian artists are noted for their coloring, they have such glorious nature to copy from.

> The scene in St. Marks square, where we went for dinner was almost as fascinating. In the center of the square the bandstand stood & was soon occupied by the army band, which discoursed the most perfect music all the evening. Miss Smith [the other female physician travelling to Van] says it is away ahead of Gilmour's & other bands she has heard. The crowd was terrific. All Venice wanders thither in the evening & of course most of the strangers within her gates there were soldiers in a dozen different costumes, man of war sailors, picturesque Albanians, beautiful women with scarves draped on their heads & carrying ever waving fans, children in all costumes & the every day man & woman, a continual stream of life & color. We sat from eight until nearly ten over our dinner & watching the people & listening to the music. The naval band played Saturday night. It's almost impossible to choose between them they are both so fine.

She found the trip from Venice to Trieste unpleasant because of hot temperatures, stuffy railcars, and bland scenery, which she compared with Windsor Junction, Nova Scotia. She put that all aside on seeing Trieste for the first time. Arriving in the evening, she described the coastal community as looking "like a crescent set with diamonds and the beautiful starlight night added additional glory." Their stay was brief, leaving little time to explore the area. Their steamer for Athens departed at four o'clock the following afternoon.

En route, they alighted at Corfu for a few hours and spent a night at Patras. Culture shock is evident in KBF's description of weighing anchor off Patras.

We were sorry to bid good bye to [the Captain of the *Nanenta*] on which we passed some of the pleasantest days since we left home. The good bye was a rather stormy one. As soon as our anchor dropped four boats shot out from the shore with five or six hard looking characters on board. They insisted upon coming up our ships sides & tied ropes to the ladder which had been let down for the port officers. Two of the ships' men cleared them off the ladder into their boats but they refused to untie the ropes. Our men then took out knives & began to cut them adrift. One of the Greeks whipped out his knife in return & looked as if he would throw it at our men but there was a little breeze & they were sent flying but in a few minutes returned & this time were allowed to come up. Among them were a few hotel porters. The rest were boatmen & idlers. Such a fight as they had over us. Each porter wanted us for his hotel & each boatman the pleasure of rowing us to the shore. The discussion waxed hot & in half a second a regular fight was going on. Two young chaps flew at each other, out came their knives & it bid fair to end rather disastrously when one of the ship's officers tore them apart. Rather violent language was used & violent handling of their persons before we were safely seated in a boat & pulling for shore. There the same gang were waiting, but a group of soldiers stood by, so they behaved very well. They followed us to the custom house which was close by. The procession halted & waited while our baggage was being examined. It was exceedingly ludicrous to stand in the middle of the street & have our trunks & other traps examined, surrounded by a group of Greeks who were more

Boats in the harbour at Constantinople. KBF was thrilled by the "perfectly enchanting" city. (NS ARCHIVES)

> interested in the contents of our trunks than were the customs men. Our hotel was just around the corner so we did not take a carriage.

An Armenian whom they met aboard, and who spoke fluent Greek, eased their way somewhat by intervening on their behalf and showing them the sights. KBF is surprised at his appearance because "[h]e doesn't look at all like what I imagined all Armenians do. I met one in Princeton last winter who was very dark. Our friend of the Nanenta is fair, almost a reddish tinge in his whiskers."

The novelty expressed in letters thus far concerning architecture and history changes tone, becoming grounded in the classical literature she knows. "Corfu is said to be the ancient Scheria, the Phaeacian Island where Alkimoos reigned & where Ulysses was cast ashore & so well cared for. We passed Ithaca this morning. We got up almost too late to see the land which Ulysses loved so well. Just a few bare & bleak looking hills remained, but our Armenian said further back it was much prettier. I was very glad I had read the 'Odyssey' or should not have known about those places & would have lost part of my enjoyment."

From Patras they travelled to Corinth and took the train to Athens. They visited Kerameikos, an area of Athens known for its Street of Tombs and for a museum housing art and artifacts. KBF marvelled at how familiar some of the objects were, such as kitchen utensils and household wares "so well preserved & modern looking one could not realize they were made in unknown times." Some of the children's toys, too, looked familiar—"little figures with hats & draperies not unlike ours & carrying fans which looked quite modern."

She described in detail each place she visited in an attempt to give her sisters a flavour of her experiences. On a visit to the sanitarium of "Escalapius" [*sic*]—not to be confused with the Sanctuary of Aesculapius at Epidaurus in the Peloponnesus—she tastes the water in the grotto, said to have healing properties. "[O]f all vile concoctions it was the worst. If a nasty taste be meritorious this water should have power to cure."

But her words fail her when, after ascending the Acropolis, she stands by the Temple of Athena Nike, near the Propylaea, and looks out over the city. She says only that it is "magnificent" and directs her sister to "Read Byron's description. I shan't try to give you one."

They embarked from Piraeus aboard a vessel she believed to be "one of the largest in the Austrian Lloyds." The first night out and the following, winds were high and she was grateful to be accommodated in a "large and airy room...otherwise I should have been seasick."

A day or so later, she got her first glimpse of "Asia," again evoking classical allusions. She described "a low smooth hill rising out of the water & as we went along there was a succession of hills each a little higher than the last. The Capt. very soon pointed out Mt. Ida. It's not much of a mountain. Then there were some cone shaped hills followed by a long low hill sinking into the famous Plains of Troy in the background, a range of smooth hills or mountains. The Plains would make a fine battle field. So many scenes in the Iliad flashed before my mind as we went by."

They reached Constantinople on August 26, 1892. "It is the most impressive city from the water we have yet seen with its domes & countless minarets & beautiful palaces on each side of the Bosphorus.... It was perfectly enchanting." The beauty of the city was tarnished somewhat by the discovery that "[q]uarantine is on almost everywhere," which meant the distinct possibility of spending the winter in the city. Her disappointment, however, was mitigated upon receiving a stack of letters from home.

Her sister Tina's letters (none of which have survived) must have reiterated concerns for KBF's well-being and perhaps expressed jealousy at KBF's descriptions of her travels. They might also have contained some reproaches about KBF abandoning any responsibility for their father's care. KBF reminded Tina that, despite the delights of her European experiences, there was hardship to come. She praised Tina for her dedication to their father and all but says it was God's will for KBF to go to Armenia.

> I'm so glad Father is interested in [my letters]. I could talk for hours & hours telling him things if I were there. I want to give you all at home as much as I can of the nice part of my trip. I have worried sometimes since

> leaving whether when Father & Dan & Ella were so opposed I should have come, but it was not because I wanted to but because it seemed right that I should come. I shall have to depend on you to do & be at home what I should have been. See what a care you have all on our family & Maxie & Katie.

KBF's experience of Greeks tussling and resorting to physical violence in order secure their patronage in Patras prepared her somewhat for the noise and activity that awaited them when their steamer dropped anchor off the coast of Constantinople. She found amusing "such noise and such gibberish" of the people who swarmed the ship in small crafts to take passengers to shore. There were no wharves at which ships could tie up in Constantinople, so ship's crew members lowered passengers over the side into waiting rowboats.

The government officials they met ashore at the customs house, however, KBF found not the least bit amusing. Inspectors took apart their luggage and gave everything a thorough going-over. They confiscated a revolver and a medical textbook from Dr. Kimball. From KBF they took a volume of Byron's poetry. Kimball's items were returned; Byron was not. His work was banned in Turkey because of his sympathy for the plight of the Armenians and for fighting with the Greeks against the Turks (during which time Byron died of malaria). Doubtless the poet would have been pleased to know of his notoriety and the notion that Turks considered his poetry sufficiently subversive to warrant confiscation. Customs officials kept the volume until shortly before KBF left the city a month later. Henceforth, she was careful to keep it concealed whenever she encountered government officials and to never read it in public as long as she was on Turkish soil.

Chapter Three

"For the first time on the journey, I cried myself to sleep"

Despite their brusque welcome at Constantinople and any concerns about having to spend the winter there, KBF's spirits were not sufficiently dampened to prevent her from exploring—and enjoying—Constantinople. She wrote a few letters to her sisters from Constantinople and Trebizond, but in her personal journal she gave her attention entirely to her surroundings, impressions, and experiences.

> Constantinople itself is divided into Stamboul (the Turkish quarter) & ancient Byzantium. Directly opposite & joined by the bridge is Galata at the waters edge & Pera at the top of the hill, where most of the Europeans live & the embassies have their town palaces. Therapia up the Bosphorous is the fashionable summer resort where a cool & pleasant breeze comes from the Black Sea. Each nationality seems to have its

own quarter. You can tell at once in passing through whether it is Turkish, Armenian, Greek, Jewish, etc. The Turkish houses all have a frame of lattice work on the lower half of the windows. Every house has iron bars across the downstairs windows to keep out robbers. I do not know whether they have day policemen in Constan—but there are night watchmen who carry ironshod staves & go along thumping them every few steps. I was rather afraid the first time I heard the sound under my windows. I did not hear the cry of fire once during my stay there, but I saw the firemen returning from a fire one day in Galata. They were stripped to the waist, bare headed & bare footed & looked fit for anything but to rush into a burning house.

There are two or three fine towers from which watchers always look & at the sign of flames on the cry "Yangun var" cannons are fired but before this is done permission must be had from the Sultan & in the meantime the fire is doing its worst. At least I've been told this. If you want to see a very interesting & extremely picturesque scene, go stroll across Galata bridge & watch the people passing & repassing. In about fifteen or twenty minutes you will have seen people from almost every nation under the heavens & as many different costumes. From end to end of the bridge there is one mass of color. You will see the Turk dressed a la Frank but of course wearing the fez, or in his costume, loose baggy trousers of fawn, gaily coloured waist or perhaps a cream one & a long coat of fawn, or of rose, dark green, etc. & a roll of white around his fez, this usually denotes the scholar or teacher. Turkish women in garments of bright red, vivid green, pink, pale blue, rich browns, black & white & usually of silk cut like a loose ulster with a long cape behind, which is drawn across the shoulders & fastened low on the bosom. The neck is filled in with lace which shows through the "Yashmak." This is of white muslin draped around the head & brought across the face so that the eyes alone can be seen. Where these garments are cut nicely they are very graceful & becoming especially those of black silk. The poorer classes do not wear silk & very often do without the cape. It's fun to see the colored women in their snow white garments which accentuate their blackness & they seem very fond of a roseen shade too, which contrasts beautifully with their complexion. Then you will see soldiers in different regimentals, sailor laddies, Greeks, occasionally in the Albanian costume, Koords [*sic*], finely formed but with wicked faces, Armenians, Persians, Arabs, gipsies, tall & slender negroes black as ebony, beggars of every description, the blind halt & the lame & you will see magnificent horses drawing carriages in which sit officers in dazzling regimentals or a closed carriage with drawn curtains in which possibly some one from the Sultan's harem is taking a drive. You will be jostled by "hamals" carrying their loads of boards, immense trunks, boxes, etc. "Hamals" are men who transport goods on their backs. They wear a leather pad to rest their burden on which alone looks heavy enough for one person to carry. It is astonishing the immense weight those men can carry & makes one sad to see men transformed into beasts of burden. One could spend hours on the bridge & be seeing new things all the time. The ferry boats all start from this point. It is very amusing to watch one getting off. Everything is done so leisurely & the people do not seem to mind if they miss their boat. They will sit down & drink coffee, smoke cigarettes or eat walnuts & be perfectly contented until the next boat goes. It's very funny the way Easterners disregard time. You will see them lying around sound asleep or sitting in the midst of dirt talking & laughing as if there was nothing else in the world to do. The Bazaars in Stamboul [*sic*] are well worth visiting. Such wonderful things are brought forth from their cubby holes & displayed before you. Elegant Brusa silks, old embroideries in dainty colours & beautiful patterns, magnificent rugs, old armour very interesting to see, native slippers of all patterns plain & embroidered. Old china & old jewelry, in fact almost every conceivable thing is there. One needs to have lots of money to spend to enjoy oneself thoroughly. We indulged ourselves very sparingly in such luxuries.

Our first sightseeing was a drive around the old walls. On our way we drove through the gate of the Sublime Porte, past the old government buildings, the mint & through a court where stands an old tree with an iron hook in it on which the Janissaries were strung up, on past the Treasury (the entrance to which we had to deny ourselves, the admission fee is high & Mr. Chambers could not get a large enough party to share the expense so that each one's admission would be reasonable) & to the museums. In the first there were some beautiful pieces of statuary in marble & bronze. A bronze Hercules struck me as being very fine, there was so much life & strength in the figure. There were several of those ancient cylinders which would be interesting to those who could decipher the inscriptions & there were bracelets, earrings, necklaces, bits of bronze etc., which Shlieman [*sic*] had found in Troy. In one room by itself stood an immense statue of Hadrian with one foot on a Greek's neck. We had to hurry through as our time was limited & we were anxious to see the wonderful sarcophagus in the other museum. It was discovered three years ago at Sidon & was then supposed to be the tomb of Alexander the Great or one of his generals & is magnificent enough to have contained a Greek God. On one side a battle is represented & it may be a continuation of it on each end. On the opposite end is a grand chase. The figures on the pediment are small but very beautiful & the colour is fresher here than elsewhere. The mouldings are perfectly exquisite. One is a beautifully carved vine & beneath is a finely cut pattern which none of us knew. The draperies of the men & the fittings of the horses were coloured in reds, blue, heliotrope & yellow, which give a striking effect. Altho the sarcophagus is encased in glass the colors are gradually fading. It is such a pity because one can get a better idea from it than from anything else, how gloriously resplendent the Parthenon frieze must have been. When the men were taking the sarcophagus from the earth they had to wear gloves & change them every few minutes so as not to soil it.... It has not yet been photographed but is to be very soon & I shall get some pictures of the most beautiful thing I have seen since I left home. We next drove through the Hippodrome & saw the Egyptian obelisk which is very old & so well preserved, & the headless snakes, a column of brass which came from Delphi, three snakes twisted into one column. The triple heads supported the golden tripod of the priestess of Delphi. It was consecrated by the Greeks in the temple after the defeat of Xerxes. It is said that Mahomet the conqueror shattered one of the heads with his battle axe as a trial of strength. One of them is in the museum & an ugly looking thing it is too. We visited Pigeon Mosque & saw the pigeons being fed. Some seeds were thrown out from the mosque & hundreds & hundreds of pigeons came flying down. They were all of one colour, a pinkish slate, & looked as pretty as they scrambled for the food.

At last we were off for the walls & soon came to the castle of the Seven Towers where we ate our lunch & then drove along by the picturesque ramparts. Besides the triple walls there was a wide ditch which is now about filled with rubbish & level with the ground. On the inside wall there are square towers at regular distances, some with gaping rents & in some places completely wrecked. It was exceedingly interesting to drive along & picture to ourselves the taking of Constantinople. The Turks had to work hard for their victory & you would think they would be anxious to preserve the walls, but instead of that, the last Sultan gave them to his mother & told her she could sell them for building material & thereby gain an income. The destruction had actually begun when the English stepped in & put a stop to it. On the other side of the road from the walls is a cemetery. For a perfect picture of desolation commend me to a Turkish graveyard. Greek & Jewish quarters to the bridge thence home.

Another time we visited the tomb of Mahomet the Conqueror. There are three tombs in the mosque each covered with dark blue velvet & heavily embroidered in silver & draped with beautiful cashmere shawls. Mahomet's is the largest & finest. His fez is placed at the head & on it there is a most superb diamond star & an ostrich plume. The tombs are enclosed by a silver rail & outside standing all around are magnificent inlaid prayer desks on which are lying beautifully illuminated copies of the Koran & on shelves in the corners are silver & inlaid boxes to keep the precious book in.

I had just a peep at St. Sophia. Mrs. Jones (one of the teachers at Stamboul) & I went alone & were told afterwards that it was a rather hazardous thing to do. We confessed to each other on coming out that we had each been a little afraid especially when the stair door was locked behind us when we went up to the gallery. You can all read a much better description of the church than I can give so I shall not say much about it. The six pillars on each side which support the dome are of green jasper. The capitals are very beautiful. The work is so delicate & the carving under the aisles & along the space above & under the balcony is like lacework. The walls are lined up with beautiful slabs of marble like St. Marks, but unlike St. Marks each slab has a moulding around it, a narrow one in the bottom & top row of small slabs & wider moulding on the large middle slabs. The mosaics are not equal to St. Marks. The floor was covered with straw matting. In winter they put rugs down.

Now I must take you over to Scutarie.... You can go on a [steamboat] or on a Caïque, the latter is the more picturesque. Caïques are long narrow boats pointed & decked at each end, usually made of light yellow wood. The seats or rather cushions in the bottom of the boat are covered with bright colours. The Caïquege [*sic*] wears a costume of white, large baggy trousers almost like a skirt & a loose blouse, red fez. It is perfectly delightful to glide along the Bosphorous in one of these shells. It is the very poetry of motion. The morning after the lecture Miss Olmstead took us down to the English cemetery [based on KBF's description, this is likely the Aşiyan Asri Cemetery, where renowned intellectuals, writers, and artists are buried]. Such a charming spot it is! So quiet & restful. One could lie on the bank by the water all day & drink in the beauty of the surroundings. To our left is a pretty little town once ancient Chalcedon. Directly in front the blue Marmara stretches & in the distance we can see the Prince Islands. On the right San Stefano runs away down to a position to meet the sea. Further up the grey walls with their embattlements then Seraglio Point & Constantinople with its many domes & dazzling white minarets from which as we look the Muizzin [*sic*] calls the faithful to prayer. "There is no God but God & Mohammed is his prophet." Then your eye sweeps up the Bosphorous with its beautiful hills on either side, covered with stately cypress & other trees, & in the ravines pretty little villages. At the waters edge pure white palaces & pretty kiosques add their quota to the beauty & over all there is a sky of the most wonderful blue. Oh! It was delightful. I wish I could do justice to it & to Constantinople in general.

Although thoroughly charmed by Constantinople, its bazaars, its history, and its people, KBF was anxious to reach her destination. After the first few days, she found it increasingly difficult to relax and enjoy herself, or to keep her attention on her first lessons in the Armenian language. Their stay extended to just over a month before they could depart for Trebizond—a five-day journey through the Bosphorus and over the Black Sea.

> It was a perfectly calm night & the water as smooth as glass. On each side of the Bosphorous the lights twinkled, pretty little villages, climbing up the slopes at the waters edge. When we passed Hizar & came near Therapia, the scene was like fairy land. It seemed like quite a large lake surrounded by a chain of villages brilliantly illuminated. The moon was just sinking behind the horizon & the stars were reflected in the quiet water. There was not a sound to be heard but the plash of water against the sides of our ship as we steamed swiftly along towards the Sea. We stayed on deck until the lights from the shore grew dim in the distance. The moon had disappeared, the stars still bright—but glittered coldly at us & we began to feel the roll of the ocean.

They woke the next morning, feeling ill though the sea appeared as calm as the previous night. KBF and her companions were unable to eat breakfast. KBF and Dr. Smith seemed to fare worse than Dr. Kimball, who finally helped them up on deck later in the morning to take some fresh air. That revived their spirits and calmed their stomachs somewhat, and by the end of the day they felt well enough to take some food.

On the same day, KBF made the acquaintance of a Turkish woman after offering her a pin to secure her yashmak (face veil) from fluttering in the wind. To thank KBF, the woman offered cigarettes and seemed hurt when KBF declined them. Undaunted and wanting to do some kindness in return, the woman wrapped up KBF as she had seen Dr. Kimball do earlier in the day, helped her to a chair, and stayed with her. Neither spoke the other's language, so they amused themselves teaching one another some words. After a while, the woman left, returning a few minutes later "with a glass of the nastiest stuff I ever tasted & insisted on me taking some of it. I took two sips & she seemed to feel badly because I would not drink it all, but it was so horrid. Just like water with kerosene oil in it. Raki I think they call it." Raki—a distilled liquor made from a combination of fruits, usually grape, fig, and plum—is an acquired taste at the best of times, but for a teetotalling young woman from Nova Scotia recovering from seasickness, it must have been quite a shock.

A small party of five American missionaries greeted KBF, Kimball, and Smith (the other women in their original travelling party having gone to other missions) at the wharf in Trebizond, waving two American flags. KBF told them that she felt "quite left out" because she was a British subject and should have been greeted by a Union Jack. Though said in jest, her words impart a patriotic streak that would emerge again a few years later during dangerous times in Van.

Their stopover was just over a month's duration, during which time they stayed two weeks with a Dr. and Mrs. Parmalee in their "great barn of a house" on a hillside overlooking Trebizond and the Black Sea, and "behind us the everlasting hills." KBF does not indicate where they moved for the rest of their stay in Trebizond, but once again, she made full use of her time, exploring the local area. After travelling so many miles by ship, train, and carriage, she enjoyed her first opportunity to get out and ride a horse again. Though stiff and sore the first couple of days, "that was nothing compared to the pleasure!" She went out each day, on one occasion visiting a local monastery carved into the rock above the city, marvelling over the paintings that graced its walls, and enjoying the "magnificent" view of the surrounding area.

As in Constantinople, local women covered up when out in public. KBF noted that women in Trebizond tended to be "even more closely veiled" and more plainly dressed than their Constantinople counterparts, wearing "as a rule a large square of blue & white check draped around them from head to foot, holding it together before their faces with their hands. It was laughable to see how quickly they drew it together when strangers appeared, just one eye peeping out."

While they were still in Trebizond, word reached them that cholera had broken out at Erzurum, one of the places where they planned to break their journey. Before being permitted to continue to Erzurum, they had to quarantine for five days at Hamsiköy. With autumn came cooler weather, and with cooler weather there were fewer outbreaks of cholera. They hoped there would be little to concern them on the last part of their journey, which they wished to complete before the harsher weather of late autumn.

Their small party of ten people set out from Trebizond at six thirty on the morning of Wednesday, the second of November. Two wagons carried their combined possessions, in one of which rode the wife, two children, and two servants of an American missionary named Chambers. He rode on horseback, as did KBF, while Dr. Kimball and Dr. Smith rode in a "little dog cart, a dainty little affair that looked out of place starting on such a journey." Rounding out the party was an armed escort or zaptieh. "He rode [a] grey horse & his suit of blue & red, belt filled with cartridges, sword hanging by his side & gun slung around his shoulders, added quite a good deal to the picture."

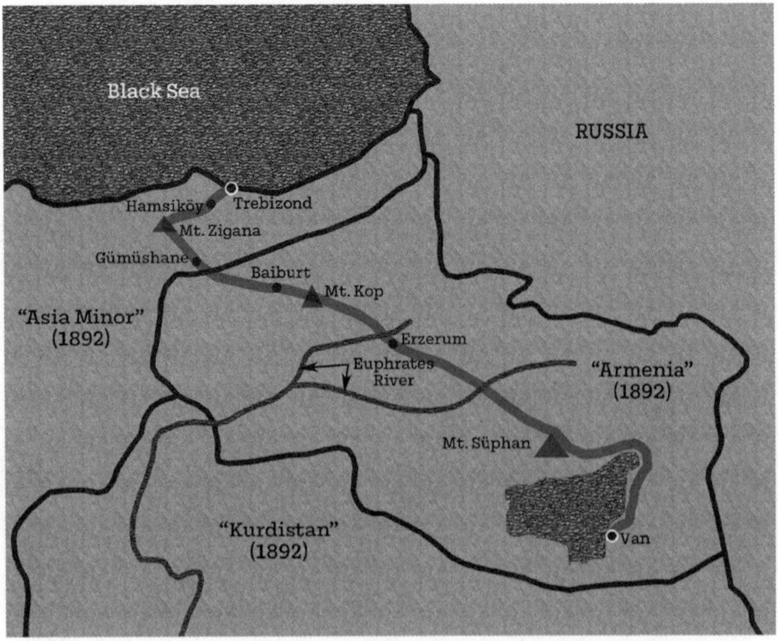

KBF's route from Trebizond to Van, November 1892.

The journey was slow and difficult, traversing harsh terrain. To make things even more challenging, there were problems with one of the wagons. As KBF explained,

> The road at first ran along between two mountain ranges [along] the very bottom but soon we began to ascend the left mountain & for two days, it ran along the side of the mountain. At our feet, a deep ravine through which flowed a stream of water. Small villages were visible all over the mountains, sometimes so high up you wondered how the people could climb to them. The first day we lunched at Jevislee [possibly Zaferli]

> 15 1/2 miles from Trebizond, elevation of 1125 ft [343 m]. At night we stopped at Kenemidler Khan [inn]. Our room was small, cold & damp.

At last they reached the quarantine station at Hamsiköy where they expected to spend five days. Shortly after their arrival, however, the station received a telegram to say that quarantine was lifted. The news boosted their spirits and energized them, moving KBF to claim that Hamsiköy was a "beautiful little village."

Their progress the next day, November 4, was hardly better than the previous one. They ascended Mount Zigana (elevation 2,032 metres). Nowadays a tunnel—one of the longest in the country—goes through the mountain. For KBF and her colleagues in 1892, there was no other way but over.

> The first two hours we travelled through a beautiful beech forest, grand old trees. Since then we have scarcely seen a tree, certainly not on our journey from Erzeroum [I believe she means Trebizond, because Erzurum still lies ahead]. The pull up Zigana was hard. We all walked as we neared the top. It was hot & our horses were tired as were we when we reached the khan at the top. The view from the point is rather fine. From it we saw the first snow-crested mountains but we were in a hurry to get on & did not stop to take it in very well. We went down to Maden Khan for lunch, ele 4100 ft [2,032 m], same level as we started in the morning. The descent was steep & the road turned & twisted & had such sharp turns that we felt very glad when we got over the worst part of it. Sometimes we were on the edge of a cliff & could look down more than a thousand

> feet into the valley below. We stopped at Ardasa that night, the lowest point on the road, 2900 ft [884 m]. Next morning [November 5] we passed through [Gümüşhane], 3650 ft [1,112 m], a fruit district & very much like the Annapolis Valley [Nova Scotia]. A freshet last year had caused great havoc through the valley & traces of it were distinctly seen. We lunched at Sordu an hour further, passed Leka [Tekke] and came to Murad Khan for Sunday, elevation 4300 [1,311 m]. Today we had 3 rooms in a new house. It was being built for the governor (at Kumar, Turkish name) of the village. There were no windows in it & the plastering was not quite dry but it was clean & we spent a comfortable day.

On November 6, they paused for a simple lunch of coffee and bread at Aşkale. They had consumed only their coffee before someone informed them of sixteen deaths from cholera in the village. They threw away the bread, and continued on.

They reached Erzurum later that day, where they "found cholera doing very bad work. Average death rate 30 to 60 per day." This was the final destination for the Chambers family and their servants.

KBF, Dr. Kimball, and Dr. Smith departed Erzurum with a servant on November 7 for the last leg of their journey in the company of Dr. Raynolds (an American physician who served in the Union army during the Civil War and whose name KBF consistently spelled as "Reynolds"), a quarantine doctor whom she does not name, and three additional zaptiehs. Dr. and Mrs. Chambers accompanied the party out of the city. They hadn't gone far when Dr. Kimball's horse balked. One of the male servants travelling with them seized the horse's bridle, and everyone feared an accident when the horse spun wildly around the man three times. When the horse tried to bolt, Dr. Chambers rode his horse in front of it and succeeded in stopping it. Thinking the party was settled, Dr. and Mrs. Chambers bade them goodbye and headed back to Erzurum. They had just disappeared from view when one of the wheels on a cart carrying their belongings became stuck. They freed it, but needed to have it fixed, so they limped along until they found a place to repair it. "We stopped just outside a village in the middle of a field & had lunch. How good it tasted. Only biscuit & chicken with one doughnut each & nothing to drink but we were so hungry we enjoyed it without tea or coffee."

KBF found the scenery not as interesting as in other points along the way, but she was fascinated with the number of forts so high up in the mountains. They encountered three zaptiehs escorting four prisoners with iron collars around their necks and chains attaching one prisoner to the next. She felt more secure knowing they had four zaptiehs in their own party, one of whom carried "a short sword and a revolver," which, she believed, made him as good as two zaptiehs.

At the end of the day they found accommodations in a stable, "a much better room than we expected. It is clean looking & plastered. We are going to have dinner, then have our beds put up & go to sleep." Dr. Raynolds arranged that the horses would be accommodated elsewhere for the night.

November 8 passed with little event, other than when one of the Arabian horses in their party became stuck fast in a mud hole. The quarantine doctor travelling with them, whom KBF didn't care for because she found him to be unpleasant and "a little bit of an old woman," became as incensed as if the horse had deliberately got itself in such a quandary. With some time and a great deal of effort, the horse was freed. After that the road was in fairly good condition, and because they

Rev. Dr. George C. Raynolds, American missionary in Van, c. 1900. Dr. and Mrs. Raynolds opened the Van mission in 1872. A medical doctor who had served in the Union army during the Civil War, Dr. Raynolds established a mission hospital in Van, but also devoted himself to evangelistic work. (PROJECT SAVE ARMENIAN PHOTOGRAPH ARCHIVES, COURTESY VART SHIRVANIAN HACHIGIAN)

were passing across a plain, no mountains had to be ascended or descended, though there were several small rivers to ford.

They stopped in another village to stay in yet another stable, but this time the horses remained.

> The stable is more like our barn at home than any thing else. Mud floor & the horses stand around anywhere. In one corner of the place a room is fitted up for travellers. It is raised four or five feet from the level of the horses & is really more comfortable than one could imagine. It is open & of course the smell from the horses is not pleasant. We entered by what looked like a door into a stone wall or cellar & walked about 100 feet through a dark alleyway & presumably came into our apartments. Miss Kimball went ahead & then came out for Miss Smith & me. How she laughed at our timidity in entering such a place. It was as warm as toast &

> we rested well that night. We visited the family of the house in a room off from the public apartment. Two women & some children sat around a hole in the floor warming themselves. Their fireplaces are called toniers, large barrel affairs sunk in the ground & lined with iron. The room was utterly bare, mud floor, etc.

Their journey the following day began with bleak weather, cold and drizzly. KBF's spirits were quite low until the party came to a steep incline. Everyone either dismounted or alighted from wagons, except for KBF who decided to risk "taking a header over my horse" and remained in her saddle. The unpleasant quarantine doctor, however, would not alight from his cart and proceeded ahead. Within seconds, the cart had tipped, dumping him unceremoniously on the ground, surrounded by hay and covered in the cart's contents. The scene greatly amused KBF and lifted her spirits as "we all laughed and laughed heartily before we even knew the man was safe."

The weather grew colder and it began to snow. While KBF enjoyed the sight of snow-topped mountains looking as if dusted with powdered sugar, "there is not much fun being along when the powdering is being done." To make things even more uncomfortable, the snow changed to rain, and it poured down. Since she and Dr. Raynolds were on horseback, they pushed ahead of the group to the next village to secure accommodations. These they found at the home of an Armenian minister, where they spent a comfortable night in preparation to resume their journey at five the next morning.

Travel the next day was pleasant, for the most part, until more rain appeared later in the day. By that time, they reached their billets in "a stable parlor in a village on the banks of the Euphrates" in a home belonging to a Turk. Their room "is the cleanest we have had gotten, nice matting on the floor and the ceiling is free of spider webs." She watched in fascination as their host took down his prayer mat and began his evening prayers. "He first finds his 'keblat' then stands with folded hands & gazes toward it & then puts his hands on his knees & bows twice, then gets on his knees & touches the floor with his forehead three times, arises & goes through the same performance several times, remaining silent the whole time, but I presume he says his prayers quietly."

At their next stop, however, KBF lost heart and reached her lowest point since leaving New York. Though she had written in a couple of letters that she felt homesick occasionally, she said that she always managed to take herself in hand so that the feeling was fleeting. Now, nearing the end of her journey and heading for a final quarantine station where she would spend ten days before continuing on to her destination, it all seemed too much: the rain, the snow, the barrenness, the dirt, the cold, all relentless. She confided in the pages of her journal:

> Am sitting in the middle of a field just outside the village where we were put up for Sunday. We found it impossible to reach quarantine. Notwithstanding, we got up at 2 o'clock yesterday morning & prepared to start. We all passed an almost sleepless night & were tired when we started but still we should have pushed forward had our baggage horses been able to keep up. The village is composed of Kurds, Turks & Armenians, the dirtiest & raggedest looking crowd imaginable & our stopping place is fearful. It is small & black with smoke, the ceiling thick with cob webs, the odor from the stable is vile. For the first time on the inland journey I cried myself to sleep & almost wished I was back in dear old Yarmouth. I dreamed all night about

> leaving home & was trying to decide whether to come or not hoping against hope that something would interfere to stop my coming. When I awoke I found I had come & a long distance too from dear home friends.

She attempted to divert her attention by doing some tasks but that, too, proved difficult, as the novelty of their presence caused quite a stir among the locals.

> Miss K., Miss S. & I after breakfast thought we would wash some pocket handkerchiefs in the brook that flows by the village & started down. We were followed by men, women & children & found it would be impossible to do the work there, so went back to the house. The women wear their hair in braids down their backs & think it a very strange thing that we do not do likewise. On their heads they wear a metal turban with small chains hanging from it on which coins are attached. Some of them wear nose rings & look barbarous with them. The small children are almost naked. Several boys & girls simply had ragged jackets—limbs perfectly bare. It was funny how curious they were about our apparel. They lifted Miss S's skirts & examined them. A small belt satchel which I wore attracted their attention as well as my ring & hair pins. When we came out to this field, the people were going to follow but Dr. Reynolds [*sic*] drove them off & now we are free from their starving eyes.

Her spirits improved the over the next few days, and she could appreciate the natural beauty around her. "Mount

Süphan [is] an extinct volcano," she wrote. "Its top is covered with snow all year round. Its foot hills look like toad stools all around it & even they are already covered with snow.... There had been a heavy hoar frost during the night & the ground was still white & glistened & sparkled as the sun shone on it."

At this point, they were three days' journey from Van. It would be another thirteen days before they reached it, however, as they were required to enter a ten-day quarantine before being permitted to enter the city. There was some comfort to be found in the knowledge that this last quarantine would be at her final destination.

Their journey continued along rocky, rutted roads over mountainous terrain, fording rivers and navigating mud holes. On crossing one river shortly before arriving at the quarantine station, one of the carts became stuck. As they worked to free it, the cart tipped, scattering its contents. And when KBF tried to cross, her horse stumbled. She was able to remain in her saddle, but her saddlebags slipped off and into the river. The only consolation was the shallowness of the river and its slow current. All the items—her underclothes, a box of provisions, and two carpets—were retrieved and spread out on the bank. The party could not wait for everything to dry out, so all was gathered up in the hope there would be facilities to dry everything at the quarantine station.

Two zaptiehs met them not far from the quarantine station near a small village (which KBF doesn't name) at the foot of Mount Süphan and kept them under close watch for the remaining hour-and-a-half of their journey. KBF likened it to being marched like prisoners. They learned there had been three thousand deaths from cholera in the area between the end of September and the beginning of November. Quarantine officials were taking no chances.

When they entered the station, no one approached them. Instead, people shouted orders at them from a distance. An official refused to accept from their hands a letter of introduction from the quarantine doctor at Erzurum. He ordered them to throw the letter on the floor. Another official approached with "a fuzzy brush and some sulphur." The man lit the brush, threw sulphur over it, then picked up the letter with tongs and held it over the smoke. Satisfied that it was disinfected, the first official took the letter and read it.

A man brought in a pan of coals and placed it in the middle of the floor. He threw sulphur over it and ordered them to approach the pan. They stood over it five minutes for fumigation. The belief that such a practice would kill cholera amused KBF. She wrote in her journal that she was relieved that they didn't stick them with penknives, as they had done to the letters forwarded to them at the station. She counted forty-three holes in one from her brother Fred.

Their accommodations were a large room with a mud floor, no windows, and no ventilation holes in the roof. They spread out some carpets on the mud floor when they realized that no raised platform would be provided for their beds. Their servant built a fire outside to cook their food because indoors there were no facilities or ventilation. There were no stalls or hitching posts for horses as there had been in other barns in which they stayed, so they tied up the horses outside. Curtains divided the men's accommodations from the women's. The prospect of spending ten days in such a place in winter weather, with not even a fire to warm them, was bleak. Shortly after their arrival, Dr. Kimball came down with a mild form of cholera, from which she recovered after only a few days. KBF came down with a chill, which she assumed was a cold. When she came down with the chills again after arriving in Van, Dr. Kimball diagnosed her with malaria. KBF suffered recurring bouts, which caused chills and neuralgia. Sometimes her symptoms were sufficiently severe that she took to her bed.

KBF's spirits lifted somewhat when the weather became warmer than it had been. Although not permitted near public places, they had access to the broad plain beside the station where they walked or rode each day. Things improved further when Dr. Raynolds put up tents in which to house the group for the duration of their stay.

Some stories she heard while in quarantine amused KBF, such as a local custom of using a "holy nail" to cure a number of ailments, including headaches. But mirth turned to indignation when she learned later about another of its applications: "[S]ome of the old church Gregorians carried a nail, supposed to be from Our Saviour's cross, through the streets [of Van] in procession to cleanse the polluted water. The nail was immersed in it & the people drank freely & as would be expected more cholera ensued."

Just after this entry, she added: "Heard of a funny case today. Miss K. & Miss S. had been attending a woman who had hysteria. At first she improved under their care but lately she took it into her head not to speak & her friends went for this holy nail & presented it before her & she immediately began to talk & of course they say 'See all the good the Protes [Protestant doctors'] medicine could do. This holy nail has made a perfect cure.'"

During quarantine, two happenings gave KBF her first insights into what life was like for the local people. She learned that an Armenian was arrested for the murder of a soldier; though it was common knowledge he was innocent, it was equally common knowledge he would hang for the crime.

And then there was the incident in which an Armenian man's wife, kidnapped by a Kurd, was living with her abductor in the village; the Armenian husband had no legal recourse to get his wife back. Such occurrences were so unfamiliar to KBF that she seemed stunned by them. Her only comment in her journal, where she safely confided private thoughts, was "The Kurds are lawless & wicked."

Chapter Four

"Don't ever put Armenia on my address"

On November 28, 1892, KBF sent a cable home to let her family know she had cleared quarantine. The move to their new accommodations in the mission compound brought a surge of activity as they settled in to their quarters. The cholera outbreak led to the closure of the mission school, so KBF and her colleagues focused their complete attention on cleaning and painting. Her first letter to her sister Tina is dated December 7 and gives no details of her journey from Trebizond; neither does it mention anything of murders or abductions. Instead, she described her daily life, her accommodations, the view of the mountain and the lake outside her bedroom window, the food, and her progress with Armenian language lessons with one Baron Nesham. ("Baron" is not an aristocratic title but rather the equivalent of "Mister.") She wanted details of home and responded to news her sister shared in the letters forwarded to Van. She promised to write a long letter each week to at least one family member to share among them all, and asked them to write weekly to her. The postscript reminded her sister, "Don't ever put Armenia on my address. The place is not recognised in Turkey officially."

At this time, the Ottoman Empire still had territory in Europe, referred to on maps as "Turkey in Europe." Constantinople was in Turkey in Europe, across the Channel of Constantinople from Scutari, in Asia Minor. Armenia was one of the three provinces of "Turkey in Asia," along with Asia Minor in the west and Kurdistan, which shared borders with Armenia in the east, then extended south to sandwich between Syria to its west and Persia to its east, including part of which is now Iraq. Van sat in the province of Armenia, near the border with Persia. Today, Armenia is a separate country, northeast of Van, which remains in Turkey.

Varak Mountain and American Missionary Compound, Van, Ottoman Empire, c. 1900. (PROJECT SAVE ARMENIAN PHOTOGRAPH ARCHIVES, COURTESY VART SHIRVANIAN HACHIGIAN)

Another view of the American Missionary buildings, including Dr. George C. Raynolds' house and the hospital, Van, Ottoman Empire, c. 1904. (PROJECT SAVE ARMENIAN PHOTOGRAPH ARCHIVES, COURTESY VART SHIRVANIAN HACHIGIAN)

The mission compound—containing a school, a hospital and dispensary, and accommodations for doctors, missionaries and their families, diplomats (British and Russian), teachers, boarding students, and a small domestic staff—stood outside the fortified walls of the old city of Van, in an area known as "The Garden City" (Aikesdan) after the orchards and groves planted by local people. Eventually, both Armenians and non-Armenians built homes in the area. Each time KBF visited a local residence, hospitality included offerings of Turkish coffee, raki, and fresh fruit from private gardens. She noted that cucumbers, in particular, seemed a particular delicacy and were often served to guests. The mission compound had gardens of its own, which, along with livestock raised and a variety of fish caught in the brackish waters of Lake Van, furnished food for residents.

A few days after Christmas 1892, KBF wrote to Tina, telling her, "I thought of you all at home [on Christmas Day] & hoped you were having a nice time." KBF was delighted to receive a cable on Christmas Day carrying wishes from home, which made her feel close to her family. Its arrival helped to dispel "a small fit of the blues" she felt that day and enabled her to not "feel half so far away after this." KBF and her mission colleagues shared a Christmas meal at the home of the missionary Frederick David Greene and his family.

Born in Turkey to American missionaries, Greene spent much of his life in Van. With the increasing violence toward Armenians, growing antagonism toward Christian missionaries, and the death of his mother in Erzurum in February 1894, Greene returned to the US with his father, wife, and son. He subsequently published a book that became influential in garnering support for the Armenian relief movement in the US. *The Armenian Crisis in Turkey: The Massacre of 1894, Its Antecedents and Significance* included letters from Van missionaries containing survivor testimony and describing injustice, acts of violence, and horrific details of the rape and murder of women and children. He kept the identities of the missionaries anonymous in order to protect them.

But at Christmas 1892, the worst of those events was yet to come. The occupants of the Van mission compound gathered together to give thanks, share food, and sing carols. There were gifts, although KBF and Dr. Kimball could not afford to give any. They had spent their own money to buy supplies for the school and hospital. KBF was touched to receive a pair of mittens and a framed picture for her room from the Greenes, and a silver pin in the shape of a bow from Dr. Raynolds.

The Armenian community followed the Gregorian calendar, so while KBF found Christmas celebrations on December

24 and 25 quiet, she plunged eagerly into activities in preparation for Armenian Christmas and New Year in January 1893, during what Dr. Kimball called, as reported by KBF in a letter to her sister, "an unprecedented cold snap." KBF helped to make small bags to fill with fruit, nuts, and cookies to distribute to the children attending the mission school. Rev. Greene provided coloured paper for the children to make decorations for the chapel. KBF helped them make "stars and crowns" to wear during the evening chapel service, while singing new hymns she had taught them. With so much to be done, the children stayed up well past their bedtime that week, in order to ensure nothing was missed.

In the midst of all the Christmas preparations, the mission also prepared for the wedding of one of their teachers, Satinug Marderoise, a few days before Christmas. The children learned a new hymn for this occasion too, and on the day accompanied Dr. Kimball, KBF, and the wife of a missionary, Mrs. Allen, to the chapel. There, they found Satinug dressed in a "silk dress and light veil" and her fiancé, "looking almost English in his swell suit of broadcloth." After the ceremony, guests retired to the groom's home to drink tea and offer "congratulations and good wishes." KBF noted that the bride's family did not attend the gathering at the groom's home, as it "was not considered proper." She further noted that she, Dr. Kimball, and Mrs. Allen were Satinug's only friends to attend an otherwise all-male gathering.

Part of the Christmas celebrations involved a visit by the priest to each family. After chanting a prayer and saying a blessing, the family paid him a small donation—"anywhere from 100 paras to five piasters"—before he left. KBF noted wryly, "If the blessing is rated according to the pay it is not thought much of."

Though committed to missionary work, she did not much enjoy entertaining visitors or keeping up with any correspondence except that which was of personal interest. She assured her sister that she would do her duty by responding to business correspondence and preparing reports. She found much of it was "rather a bore...[but] it's all in the work so I shall do it cheerfully." In the early days, when she could not converse in Armenian, she found social calls particularly trying.

> There were so many callers to take up our time & altho' I could not talk to them, I had to sit & give them an occasional smile which was the best I could do. They stay about an hour each call & sometimes longer & it is the custom to give callers tea or coffee. If tea, each person must have two cups & it's a perfect bore, not to say a little bit distressing, when one has to drink with all the callers. They take up a great deal of one's time, but I suppose that is part of our work, to be always ready to receive the people, but when I get in my own room I mean to do more studying & not always come out when callers arrive.

Her cozy room was her retreat, which she was both relieved and happy not to have to share with anyone. She described the room as sparsely furnished with items belonging to the former occupant, a Miss Ellen Ladd who had travelled to America to marry a Van missionary, Rev. Herbert Allen of Bangor, Maine, and was expected to return with her husband the following year. KBF's few personal effects helped to make it feel homey. She vowed to save money from her meagre salary over the winter to buy furniture of her own so she could return the borrowed items to her absent colleague when she returned.

On a table in one corner of her room stood a family photo album. She was grateful that photography was invented before she travelled halfway around the world, so that she could carry her loved ones' images with her and send them photos of her travels. To her delight, a letter received early in 1893 contained recent pictures of some family members. The "little sunbeams" included photos of KBF's father, her sisters Tina and Edith, and a tintype of a niece, Maxie. KBF tucked Tina's photo in the corner of her mirror so "I have to smile back every time I see you." Missing in her collection was another niece (and her namesake), Kate, and one of their late mother of whom KBF would "so like something that looks at all as she used to."

Winter weather frequently blocked roads, making the flow of mail sporadic. Postal delivery that normally took twenty days slowed to forty. Weeks went by when KBF received no mail from home, which affected her mood. In several letters she reproached her sister for not living up to the commitment to write each week and in others wondered if her letters were being misdirected or intercepted. When the mail finally brought several letters, KBF's joy is palpable in the effusive thanks she wrote in her replies.

KBF's initial responsibilities were to learn Armenian, to teach a music class, and to care for the fifteen girls boarding at the school. Armenian teachers who also boarded at the school assisted KBF with the supervision of the boarding girls. The accommodations for the Armenian teachers "are entirely apart from ours and they have a cook to prepare their meals. Their food is very different from ours and much cheaper costing about two and a half piastres a day, or ten cents or thereabouts."

KBF was content with her responsibilities, and Baron Nesham praised her rapid progress in learning to speak Armenian. As time went by, her teaching load increased. And as the demand for the services of the two female physicians, Kimball and Smith, increased, KBF assumed administrative duties for the school and hospital. The undertaking of these responsibilities and the thoroughness with which she executed them would have a direct bearing on her being asked to undertake the organizing of nine thousand Armenian refugees in Varna, Bulgaria, in the autumn of 1896.

KBF made it a point to venture out every day, unless the weather was extremely bad. "It isn't as much fun when one has to go for exercise. It is quite necessary to get out every day and the walking is usually too bad." Dr. Kimball owned a horse but was reluctant to ride. "She doesn't like riding very much and is rather afraid of" the horse, whose name was Bobba. KBF thought the problem was that Dr. Kimball found the horse "too lively," because Kimball was unable to exercise it each day. The two women came to an arrangement. For the price of feed, KBF received the use of the horse for the winter. KBF's regular use of Bobba would break it in, and by spring Dr. Kimball would have a biddable mount. KBF hoped that, by spring, she would have sufficient funds to purchase her own horse.

KBF's tone was again irritable and reproachful in a letter dated February 16, 1893. She hadn't had a letter from any of her sisters since December and wondered whether any of hers to them were getting through. But there was another reason for irritation. A friend in Yarmouth sent a copy of their local paper. In it appeared one of KBF's letters, sent from Venice. An editor's note indicated the letter was one of a series being published in the *Halifax Herald*. KBF wrote her sister that her letters were meant "for dear friends," not the general public, and demanded to know who had sent the letters to the newspaper. Indeed, who had given them permission to publish them? But KBF also felt somewhat conflicted. If the *Herald* saw fit to publish the letters, she couldn't un-publish them, so if something good was to come of it, then she should at least be compensated for their publication. She was in straitened circumstances, and the funds would come in handy. Even so, it galled her to think of her private letters being perused by strangers.

> The punctuation was so bad that the whole sense was changed and Venice and Trieste items were completely twisted. But if the Herald considered them worth publishing, they ought to pay for them. I told Miss Kimball about it, and she says I ought to charge them ten dollars a letter and certainly not to let it drop without looking into it. She says that any paper that is worth anything would gladly pay that much.... They were my letters. If they publish them without any consent, I can charge them any price I wish and they would have to pay it. Let me know how it came about and if I can get anything for them. I should be very glad, only I should have liked to fix them a bit before coming out in the papers. Miss Kimball was almost as indignant as I, but she thinks that perhaps it will give me some money to buy some rugs. I am very doubtful myself and am sure that the Herald will pay no ten dollars a letter, but they ought to pay something. I don't know anything about such things, but she says letters of that kind are considered valuable. The Halifax Herald letter was so twisted and the thought that the others were probably as bad kept me from sleeping half the night. Please write me at once and tell me all about it. I do wish my consent had been first asked.

Despite her indignation, KBF was surprised to learn that her letters appealed to the public, though she said in a subsequent letter that she would give up on the idea of seeking financial compensation for publication. Over the next few years her initial reluctance and timidity gave way to the dawning realization that publication of her first-hand experiences was a powerful tool in the fight against the horror and brutality unleashed on the Armenian people. Her desire to tell the rest of the world of the atrocities and to garner support for Armenian aid would overtake her aversion to the spotlight, leading a few years later to more articles for the papers and public presentations in the United States. She would even take risks, while still living in Armenia, to get her words to the international press.

This change was subtle, yet distinct. When she arrived in Armenia, she was a young woman relatively ignorant of the world and informed by untested ideals. Within a couple of years that are short in terms of linear time and endless in terms of human suffering, she witnessed events that were previously unimaginable—more than the poverty and want she was told to expect. Such affronts to her notions of justice and human decency shaped her and gave her credibility and a voice to speak passionately about these crimes against humanity. Even so, she did not point fingers of blame at all Turks or all Kurds for the suffering of the Armenians, knowing that the circumstances were complicated and the history long. Not all missionaries were capable of seeing nuances and subtle distinctions. And in some cases, their actions contributed to making the situation worse, escalating the threats to the safety of missionaries themselves.

Chapter Five

"The medical work is increasing"

Since arriving in Armenia, KBF had heard tales of violence and murder, but she did not know anyone who had experienced it first-hand. In early March 1893, that changed with the death of a young man named Moses, a graduate of their school to whom they offered employment as a teacher. Moses's father was one of the wealthiest Armenian merchants in Van, who had loaned money to a Kurdish sheik. When the sheik did not repay the funds within the period agreed, the merchant travelled with an attendant to the Kurd's home. There he was received, in keeping with local traditions of hospitality, "cordially and kept all night leaving in the morning with fair promises from the Kurd." But not long after setting out the following morning, the sheik and some of his men intercepted the merchant and his attendant, shooting the merchant in the back. The terrified attendant escaped, fleeing to Van to get help. When they arrived at the scene, however, they found the Armenian had been hacked to pieces.

Moses left the school and returned home to his anguished mother. The dead man's family went to the British vice consul (noted only as "Mr. D" in KBF's journal), who convinced the authorities to arrest the sheik. But under the law, Armenians could not testify in court as witnesses. Given that the only witness was an Armenian, the sheik was eventually released to return to his home.

Sometime after his release, the sheik visited a village near Van with an entourage. While there, a group of Armenians attacked the Kurds, fatally shooting one. Zaptiehs subsequently arrested several Armenians, including Moses. Knowing who Moses was, the sheik accused him of firing the gun that killed the Kurd. The accused languished for some time in prison before being called to trial. But just before the trial began, Moses became gravely ill. He was released and allowed to go home, where he died a short time later.

Moses's younger brother carried meals to Moses during his incarceration and claimed he had seen the jailer mix something in the food before taking it to the prisoner. When two other prisoners died of a similar illness, the assumption was that the jailer had poisoned them. And when it was discovered that the jailer was a Kurd related to the man shot by the Armenians, the missionaries were sure that Moses had been poisoned. But there was nothing they could do. Like the Armenians, they had no legal rights under Turkish law. In an even greater affront, Moses's family was forced to give their possessions to the family of the murdered Kurd as reparation for Moses's alleged crime, leaving Moses's family destitute.

KBF recalled another incident that occurred while they were in quarantine. A group of Turkish soldiers arrived at the village nearby, at the foot of Mount Süphan (KBF never names the village), and asked the Armenians for a meal. In the custom of hospitality whereby a traveller need only ask to receive such support, a meal was prepared. But when it was served, the Turks demanded chairs, refusing to sit on the ground like "common Armenians." When none could be produced, the soldiers ordered the Armenians to get down on the floor to be their chairs. KBF expressed shock that one human being could do that to another without regard for the humiliation it caused.

The enmity between the Turks and Kurds on the one hand and those two nationalities and the Armenians on the other had grown steadily over the two years prior to KBF's arrival in Van. As early as 1885, when the Armenakan Party formed in Van and held secret meetings in an underground burrow used for pressing grapes, local Armenians knew they had to find a way, if not to fight back outright, then at least to draw a line. Two years later, in Geneva, the formation of the Hunchak Party by a group of Russian Armenians with strong socialist principles rooted in Marxism provided a vocal and centralized voice to Armenian oppression in Turkey.

In 1891 and 1892, members of the Hunchak Party went to Van to help organize protest and resistance to the feudal system there. A system of double taxation, whereby the mostly agrarian communities in the area paid taxes both to the Turkish government and to Kurdish agas (chieftains) was not sustainable. Entire Armenian communities lived in poverty, unable to grow food for their own people. Missionaries tried to ease things by providing bread, but they could not keep up with the demand. To add insult to injury, the requirement by Armenians to give shelter to Kurds over the harsh winters meant that not only was food diverted from Armenian "hosts" to Kurdish "guests," girls and women of the household risked rape and abduction by these "guests." Refusal by the females or non-compliance from the men often meant death.

None of these "big picture" details appeared in the pages of KBF's journal initially. Some emerged later as footnotes to individual attacks over the coming months. And what details she did know in these early days she confided to the journal's pages and discussed with her colleagues, Dr. Kimball and Dr. Smith. In contrast, KBF's letters home continued to describe daily routines, share amusing anecdotes, and ask questions about home and the specifics of events shared in previous letters. The only hint that she and her colleagues experienced any difficulties with the government occurred when KBF wrote that Dr. Kimball was not permitted to practice medicine. The problem initially arose because Kimball's medical diploma was not signed. She assured the authorities that this was only a formality easily corrected, and she was permitted by the vali (the governor) to continue to practice. At least one of the vali's wives was Kimball's patient.

As time went on and the Sultan grew impatient with the presence and the efforts of the many missionaries in Turkey, more obstacles arose for Kimball. The vali notified her in January 1893 that, because she was a woman, she should not be permitted to practice medicine. Her training was better put to use for women only; as such, she could practice as a midwife. Knowing that her grateful Armenian patients would never report her to Turkish government officials, both Kimball and Smith gambled and continued to practice medicine, though Dr. Raynolds, the mission's male physician, was always around in the event someone came asking questions.

KBF continued to suffer malaria attacks throughout 1893. In a letter to her sisters dated March 11, 1893, she reported that she'd had her first attack since the previous year. Not long after, on March 23, she wrote in her journal that she was having another attack. On September 3, 1893, she wrote to one of her sisters of an attack that seemed more severe than the chills and neuralgia she associated with malaria: "I have quite recovered from my malaria attack. It took my flesh off me. I was so proud of being fat and now I am so thin as usual." In December she took a "heavy dose" of quinine to combat an attack, causing her ears to ring "merrily." A week later, she gave her sister some advice:

> My neuralgia has entirely disappeared and I am feeling very well. I am going to send you a prescription for those iron, strychnine and arsenic pills. They make the best tonic I ever took. When you feel weak and tired, take one after each meal for about a fortnight and you will find a wonderful difference. Keep them always on hand. Now remember you must take them. Dr. Smith said she would write the prescription. Dr. Smith says the prescription is for 80 pills. Don't lose it. She says drink quite a little water after taking the pill. I want you to try them and let me know. They are much better than iron, plain and simple, and one so easy to take.

KBF's letters throughout March and April 1893 are filled with queries about people at home, their health, spring floods in Nova Scotia, and domestic purchases. KBF expressed concern upon learning that Tina had purchased a parlour organ and wondered if the payment plan over two years would be too much for Tina's budget. KBF wished she could help with the payments but reminded her sister that missionaries do not earn much. Besides, she was still trying to pay off the supplies purchased on her arrival in Van while simultaneously saving to purchase her own horse. At the end of April 1893 she delightedly told her sister that she had achieved her goal and found one, "dark brown with black mane and tail. Very pretty, spirited, but gentle and very obedient to the bit.... The horse cost 9 liras. $4.40 [in] a lira, $39.60. Very little for a valuable horse, don't you think? He would be at the least a two or three hundred dollar horse at home."

She had little time left to get used to the horse. After a long winter in which weather didn't permit much riding, KBF had to get her muscles back in shape for a five-day trip to Bitlis at the end of May for a one-week stay to attend the annual meeting of missionaries in that city.

A few days before she mentioned the anticipated trip in a letter to her sister, there were more incidents that KBF did not hint about to Tina, except to say that "[t]he medical work is increasing every day and [Dr. Kimball] and [Dr.] Smith are kept very busy." Her journal, however, tells more.

On the night of May 19, 1893, six Kurds murdered four young Armenian men and raped three young Armenian women in alleged retribution for a disagreement over sheep and grazing areas a year before. Four Kurds escaped; two others were arrested. The young women were under great pressure by the authorities to say that the men arrested had nothing to do with the crime. KBF believed that, even if the case went to trial, the accused would be acquitted given that there were no witnesses who could testify.

Around the same time, there occurred the murder of a young Armenian man named Jacob—shot in the head by another Armenian for spying on behalf of the Turks. The Armenians had reason to believe Jacob gave to Turkish authorities the names of several Armenians arrested in the death of a Turkish soldier. Officials allegedly poisoned the young Armenians, and a family member of one of the deceased killed Jacob in retribution. Though the deaths of Armenians were of little concern to authorities, the vali did not want word getting back to Constantinople. He ordered the closure of the street in which Jacob had died (presumably to remove traces) and directed that all mail be intercepted and read in order to contain news of the event. Of this event, KBF wrote in her journal, "A Kurd who came for medical advice from our Drs. in talking with one of our servants said, 'We have orders from the gov't to persecute the Armenians. Kill them if necessary.' They aren't slow to carry out these orders, as we hear of terrible outrages almost every day."

KBF made her first trip to Bitlis at the end of May. The outward journey was somewhat marred by Mr. Greene, whom KBF described to her sister in an earlier letter as having a tendency to act "very childishly" at times. On the trip to Biltis, KBF complained that he worried too much, making everyone else miserable. She reported that, by comparison, the Greene's infant son, Phillips, "was a perfect little traveller and gave no trouble," although Mrs. Greene found the trip tiring. They enjoyed good weather for three of the four days of the trip. On the last day, a downpour forced KBF to ride "under my umbrella, gossamer and rubber blanket," making the final day one of "far from pleasant riding."

Bitlis is surrounded by mountains and sits where "five valleys [run] into one centre." In her journal KBF noted:

> Situation exceedingly picturesque, streets narrow & hilly paved with stone, houses built of stones, walls or fences of same material. Iron bars are in every house window, making them look like prisons.
>
> The boys & men almost all wear dark blue baggy pants, bright girdle & shirt. A few dress a la frank & the women all are closely veiled when on the street. Some of them wear pants about the house.

> In the villages on the way to Bitlis many striking costumes were seen. Those of some of the men were very gorgeous. The women wear long red pants to the ankle, then a skirt. It looks as if one of ours had been turned up & pinned behind. Over this is worn a square apron beautifully worked in very fine cross stitch of coloured wools & silks, sometimes ornamented with beads. They wear on the head a metal cap with coins dangling down at the side.
>
> In the villages one notices more charms on the children than in Van (although here we can see many). They have blue beads sewn on the front of their caps & on the sides. Then on the sides of the shoulders back & breast as well as several strings of coloured beads on the neck & arms. The larger children have nose rings, all the girls, big & little, wear ear rings.
>
> One (in Van also) never sees a woman standing idle or at least rarely. She is almost sure to have her spinning with her & uses the old distaff of the Fates.

Notably absent in her journal description of the headdress and nose rings is the word "barbaric," which she used in an earlier letter to Tina to describe them. Perhaps she included such descriptors to convey to Turkish officials who might intercept her letters that she had little regard for the Armenians. Her journal, however, was strictly personal and a place to record her impressions, though she planned to share it with her sisters when she returned home. In the meantime, KBF wrote Tina that she preferred Van by far "for beauty and for everything else."

While in Bitlis, she stayed at the home of George Cushing Knapp, a missionary, and his wife, Alzina Churchill Knapp, a teacher. Their daughter Grace taught at the mission school in Bitlis. A few years later, a short visit by Grace to KBF and her colleagues in Van became an extended stay when massacres made travel too dangerous. In 1919, Grace Knapp wrote a memoir of her Bitlis birthplace, the massacres that occurred there between 1892 and 1896, and the genocide of 1915, entitled *The Tragedy of Bitlis*.

On the return journey to Van a few weeks later, KBF caught her first glimpse of Mount Ararat, widely believed by Christians to be the resting place of Noah's ark.

> Coming home I had my first view of Ararat. The scene at that point was magnificent. We were about descending one of the numerous mountains when Mr. Green [*sic*] called out to look at old Ararat. At our feet there was a pretty little village almost buried in trees, peeping out from under the brow of the mountain. Then the glorious blue lake that rippled and sparkled in the sunlight. Sipan [*sic*] half covered with snow on the left shore, and away, away in the distance a cone-shaped cloud of billowing white, the venerable mountain stood. I shan't soon forget the exquisite beauty of it all.

In June, not long after returning from Bitlis, she wrote in her journal that eighteen Armenian families had converted to Islam in exchange for living tax-free for fifteen years. There is no mention of this event in surviving letters home.

Given the significant difference between the Armenian and English languages—right down to a different number of characters in each alphabet—the time deemed necessary to become conversant in Armenian was two years. KBF worked hard at learning the language and was delighted when, after a few short months, she could understand what was said to her, even if she was not yet able to respond. Baron Nesham found her a keen pupil and told her she "was progressing…'palleably.' He gets his English words rather mixed at times, but I like him as a teacher." Doubtless her fondness for Nesham inspired her to learn. She sought out opportunities to listen to the language and began to attend Armenian church services.

Even before a full year passed, in August 1893 KBF was sufficiently conversant in Armenian that she could visit the homes of her pupils. She was aghast at the degree of poverty she encountered. At one home, she noted that the eldest daughter seemed bright but would not be permitted to attend school. At sixteen, her family considered her too old for school. Instead, a marriage match would soon be made for her.

KBF's letters convey she had no concern about her own marriage prospects. She doubted she would ever "get off the old maids list" and was content to devote herself to her work. Besides, she didn't understand all the fuss and expense of weddings. There are hints that she might have had admirers. In one letter, she told her sister that she had received a letter from a Mr. Moses in Yarmouth, telling her that Tina had forwarded some of KBF's letters to him. She scolded Tina and told her not to do so again. "You must remember it will make a good deal of talk in Yarmo for nothing."

The nearby monastery, or vank, rested on the slope of Mount Varag overlooking the city of Van nine kilometres to the northwest. On holy days, Armenians travelled to the monastery Varagavank, built as a necropolis in the ninth century by Seneqerim-Hovhannes, the Armenian king of Vaspurukan. Eventually the vank became the seat of the archbishop of the Armenian Church and was renowned as a great monastic centre. By the time KBF lived in Van, the vank had a modern

Armenian monks and boys with throne of King Senekerim-Hovhannes of Vaspurakan at Varagavank Monastery, Van, Turkey, c. 1880.
(LIBRARY OF CONGRESS, LC-DIG-PPMSCA-04450)

Varagavank in 1893. The monastery at Varak was partially destroyed during the massacres, and all but demolished during the 1915 genocide.
(WIKIMEDIA COMMONS)

school offering classes in theology, geography, music, and Armenian history and culture.

In July 1893, the vali decreed that Armenians were no longer permitted to visit Varagavank. According to KBF, once denied access, "they spend their time on the street corners cursing the Turks and getting drunk." Though she disapproved of their behaviour, she felt sympathy for their frustration. Not long after the decree, the vali sent seventy soldiers to Varagavank to "seize everything that is worth while. It is such a wicked shame because they had some valuable things up there, old manuscripts, etc." She felt the "unspeakable acts" sanctioned by the vali would provoke open rebellion. Three years later, Turkish soldiers returned to Varagavank to sack and rob it again, killing both teachers and students in the process. And during the 1915 genocide, Varagavank would be all but demolished. All that remains today are fragments of walls.

The government banned Armenians from owning weapons, but they were available on the black market and hoarded in private stashes or concealed by young Revolutionists in caves or pits in fields. One day, while checking on their stash and cleaning weapons, the revolver held by one young man accidentally discharged, killing another. Panicked, the Revolutionists buried the body by the river and returned to their homes. Distraught and guilt-ridden, they felt compelled to tell the young man's mother about her son's death. Beside herself with grief, she told some church elders. KBF doesn't record that one of the elders went to the authorities, but she reports that they found out regardless. Turkish soldiers retrieved the body, then arrested and imprisoned fifteen young Armenian men.

Around the same time, KBF learned of another young Revolutionist who sought to purchase a revolver. Someone directed him to an "old Turk" who wished to sell a revolver in the public market, "which was his right." The eighteen-year-old Revolutionist arranged to meet him in a quiet alley. Instead of producing the cash, however, the young Armenian tossed a handful of sand in the Turk's face, temporarily blinding him. The young man got away with the revolver, but the Turk went to the authorities. A few days later, authorities arrested the young man, who claimed innocence. In the meantime, however, the father of the perpetrator found the revolver concealed in their home and urged his son to give up the weapon in the belief that such honesty would not be punished. But the young man's friends threatened to kill the father if he breathed a word. Regardless, Rev. Greene advised the father to give up the revolver, promising to intervene with authorities on the son's behalf. Upon learning of his father's actions, the young man cursed him and refused to see him. KBF does not record the young man's fate, but given the harsh treatment meted out by Turkish authorities to any suspected of colluding with or belonging to the Revolutionist movement, we can make an educated guess.

An incident KBF recorded in her journal and included in a letter to Tina involved a disagreeable quarantine doctor, Lubvitz. Knowing that Kimball and Smith were vulnerable both because they were women and because they ignored the ban on the practice of medicine by women, the doctor—who was neither Turk nor Kurd nor Armenian—spread rumours about them. In one he claimed that, during a house call to the wife of a high-ranking Turkish official, Dr. Kimball's servant was tied up in a room while Dr. Kimball and Dr. Smith were subjected to a humiliating assault (possibly even raped) by Turks. KBF felt particularly indignant at the preposterous story, in part because Kimball and Smith enjoyed good relationships in the community, where they were "treated with all the honour possible" and also because such stories terrified the young students in their charge, who often feared going out in the event of attack.

The rumours reached the vali's ears but not before the quarantine doctor overstepped his bounds by insulting an elderly Turk who sought the doctor's assistance for his sick wife. Upon completion of treatment, Lubvitz demanded an exorbitant sum from the Turk, a man of very modest means. The doctor refused to adjust his fee in keeping with the old man's circumstances, and the man scraped together the funds to pay the bill. A few days later, however, the doctor rode on horseback from the Garden City to the Old City. The old Turk crept up on him from behind, pulled the doctor from his horse, and beat him. A crowd gathered to watch the proceedings. Authorities arrived and dispersed them but not before warning all of them not to testify if called upon.

Dr. Lubvitz brought charges against the Turk and was mortified when he turned up in court to find not one witness to support his prosecution. The case was dismissed, but Lubvitz's ill fortune was not over. To add insult to injury, the vali took exception to Lubvitz's arrogant behaviour and considered whether he should expel him from the country. KBF's journal does not indicate Lubvitz's fate.

The winter of 1893–94 was especially harsh, not just in terms of cold weather and snow. The arrest in Constantinople of a member of the Hunchak Party for distributing weapons to Armenians in the area triggered a violent sequence of events over several months. Sultan Abdul Hamid II ordered nomadic Kurds, led by the fanatically anti-Armenian sheik of Zeilan, to invade the areas of Sasun and Moush with a few thousand Kurds. After the mutasarrif (the governor of the region) claimed the Armenians were in revolt, hundreds of Armenians sought shelter in the mountains for the winter.

February 1894 brought more bad news: the death from pneumonia of Rev. Greene's mother in Constantinople. KBF wrote in her journal: "She had always been so well we could not think that a first attack of illness would carry her off. I shall always remember her as being the first to think that possibly I might be lonely in this land of the Sultan. Spent a week with her in Cnstpl & was treated so nicely. Was ill during my stay & she petted me & was as motherly in every respect. I sympathise very deeply with her children."

This, along with the death from typhoid of Dr. Smith's brother in the US a month earlier and the deteriorating circumstances in Turkey, led to decisions by both Greene's family and Smith to leave Turkey to return to the US as soon as weather conditions permitted. Though Dr. Smith thought she would remain in the US only for a few months until satisfied her parents were through their initial grief, KBF and Dr. Kimball were certain that she would decide not to put her parents through the anguish of seeing their only surviving child return to an area of such grave instability and danger. Though they understood, they also realized that Smith's departure would leave them short-handed at a time when the need for services continued to grow. (Both KBF and Kimball expressed surprise and mild disapproval when Smith married a "sea captain" about a year later. Neither stated the reasons for their opinion of the match.)

The marriage in February 1894 of another teacher, Aghavne, brought reason to celebrate. Unlike the wedding of her colleague that took place during Christmas, Aghavne's would be in the Gregorian (Armenian Orthodox, or Armenian Apostolic) Church, and therefore a much more elaborate affair. KBF described the wedding in great detail in her journal and at some length in a letter to her sisters. Given KBF's opinion about the fuss and expense of weddings expressed in an earlier letter, she had little time for this one. Still, she was curious about the ritual that subordinated the bride to the groom and his sisters and required Aghavne to stand for considerable periods of time, often "in a corner."

A half-dozen boys arrived and sang "an air that would make the gayest person sad," signalling the bride to move from an anteroom to a public area in which the groom's sisters awaited her tribute of kneeling before them and kissing their hands. Guests drank tea and raki and toasted the bride. Then came the lighting of candles (one "six feet tall and three inches thick, and adorned with the most gorgeous wax flowers"), chanted choruses, and murmured blessings. During the observances, Aghavne endured "[a]nother period of standing in the corner."

Next, the groom's brother came forward to lead Aghavne to a courtyard for the next phase of the ceremony. There, she sat on a rug where her groom, Baron Mehetar, joined her after he was led in. The priest and some boys chanted more choruses, followed by more blessing and finally by three girls who approached the couple to deliver "eulogistic recitations." Afterwards, the bride and groom returned to the public room where the bride again stood for a time while her husband sat, before he directed her to join him while tea, raki, and cake were served.

KBF was stunned to learn the observances were not at an end. Carriages arrived to take guests to the church for another ceremony that lasted about an hour. Afterwards, guests shared a meal with the newlyweds. KBF and her colleagues were used to taking their evening meal at five o'clock, but the wedding meal was served at seven o'clock—seven hours after the commencement of the ritual. At this point, KBF simply wished to go home but also didn't want to seem impolite. Although many were well in their cups by the time the meal ended, KBF and her colleagues attended the room set aside for the men "to hear some native music & see some dances, both quite pretty." But all the men smoked, and KBF found the room stifling. Her gratitude "to go out into the glorious air and home" doubled when she learned her presence was not required for the further two days of celebrations.

A few days after the wedding came another grim reminder of the brutality and danger lurking around them. Officials executed the young Armenian man initially sentenced to ninety-nine years in prison for the death of a Turkish soldier the previous year. Locals believed that others arrested with him, including his father and brothers, died from poison administered to them by guards. The young man was hanged in Van's public square near Government House, and the vali ordered that the body remain hanging for three days as an example to any who would defy the government. KBF, sickened not as much by the hanging as the "barbarous" decision to leave the body as a gruesome deterrent, wrote in her journal: "One cannot blame the Turks for hanging an occasional Armenian... as a good lesson...[because] when a man gets into trouble it is because he has been plotting against the gov't & his neighbour betrays him." She wrote this on February 16, 1894, when she still believed, naively, that if everyone simply obeyed the law they would be left alone—before government-sanctioned killings escalated over the next few months to the annihilation of entire villages after the rape and torture of inhabitants, regardless of age or sex.

Although KBF—like many people of the time—accepted that punishment for some crimes required the death penalty, she found intimidation reprehensibly cruel. The vali determined that hanging the young man wasn't enough. He wanted to make sure that those who he believed would spread the message of deterrence were on hand to witness the hanging. But simply delivering a command for these witnesses to appear wasn't his style. He preferred a more novel approach.

He sent four zaptiehs to the home of an old Armenian man before dawn on the day of the hanging. Once warned by the vali that he was under suspicion of being "an enemy of the government," the old man knew he was closely watched. The zaptieh who hammered on his door before daybreak told him the vali demanded his presence. Petrified but persuaded by his family not to resist, the old man accompanied them to Government House. Upon reaching the post office he saw four zaptiehs on horseback, leading him to believe he was about to be banished from the country. The group proceeded and, a little further on, encountered a brass band. Perplexed, the old man wondered whether his banishment was to be accompanied by some sort of parade. On reaching the public square, the old man's legs gave out when he saw the scaffold. Enjoying his reaction, some Turks he knew who were in on the "joke" gravely tut-tutted, "Poor old thing." But the sick game wasn't over. They led him to the vali, before whom he cried out for a quick death—whereupon the vali burst out laughing and told him he was only to witness the hanging, not die himself. One can imagine the man's relief being great enough to make him almost faint—then his horror when he realized in a split second that he would have to watch a young man die.

In the crowd that gathered to watch the young Armenian hang was a young Turkish man of sixteen. Afterwards, he returned home greatly agitated and described the horrific scene in great detail to his mother. Not long after, his mother left the house to run some errands. "She returned half an hour later to find her only child hanging before her, dead." KBF struggled to make sense of why "a boy so old could have been so foolish."

One can only imagine his horror and distress at the execution of a young man his own age and his hopelessness for the future in a place where violence and murder were commonplace and where justice was impossible to find.

In March 1894, the problem of Dr. Kimball's unsigned medical diploma arose again when the vali sent word to the British consul in Van that all foreign physicians practicing medicine in Turkey had to forward their medical diplomas to the medical college in Constantinople for verification and approval. Dr. Kimball was understandably uneasy. First, it appears she did not provide her diploma when first asked for it a year before. Second, she was a female physician in a country where women could not practice medicine. Had she been in the US, her credential could be verified simply by contacting the Woman's Medical College in New York. In Turkey, however, the process was much more complicated. Even with the verification of her credential by the institution that granted it, there was no guarantee Kimball would be permitted to continue to practice medicine. Dr. Kimball forwarded her diploma, as commanded. Concerned lest the Sultan issue a precipitous decree to stop them practicing medicine and to shut down the dispensary, Kimball and KBF removed "quite a supply of drugs" from the dispensary and hid them in their rooms.

The developments in the Greene and Smith families changed Grace Kimball's plans to return to Boston herself in April 1894. Although she wished to return to the US to garner more financial support for the mission's work, the continuing uncertainty about whether Turkish officials would let her practice medicine made her reluctant to leave. She suspected that if she left Turkey, she would not be permitted to return. Knowing that the Greenes and Smith were about to leave made up Kimball's mind to remain, at least for the time being. KBF noted in letters and her journal that she was concerned that Kimball worked herself too hard and might collapse from the stress. There was little choice for any of them. They could leave the country, or they could remain and do as much as humanly possible; there was no in-between.

Though conditions in the country deteriorated for Armenians throughout 1894, with arms continuing to flow into Armenian hands and frequent attacks and reprisals, the mission continued its work. The doctors (Kimball and her male colleague, Raynolds) continued to see patients, and the school opened in the fall after a summer recess. But the suffering of people around them increased. KBF noted that the system of double taxation ruined two leading Armenian merchants in Van. They approached Kimball to ask for ration coupons for bread. In an effort to help preserve their dignity, she denied them relief and instead bought them an oven so they could make bread to sell.

Kimball's gesture, however, was the proverbial bandage on a sucking chest wound. KBF observed that the list of people requiring relief grew at an alarming rate, topping one hundred by March 1894. In just over eighteen months that number would grow to over four thousand—and that tally did not include the forty-five hundred who provided labour such as sewing and shoemaking in exchange for food. Some of the fine needlework produced fetched good prices in England, which helped to buy supplies needed for relief work. As long as product could move from Turkey to Europe and cash and goods could flow back to the mission in Turkey, all was well. But the precariousness of the political situation meant that, over time, even those lines would be closed.

Normally, warmer spring temperatures brought bounty from gardens. But now produce became currency to pay exorbitant taxes. Bread—a staple of the diet—was scarce because there was no grain to mill into flour. Bakeries closed. As they did so, more people starved. Most of those on the mission's relief list were women and children whose husbands and fathers were dead. "The outlook is not bright," wrote KBF. "I do not know what we are going to do when our poor fund is exhausted. Dr. Kimball who has charge of it is greatly troubled at her inability to do more for the very poor."

To make matters even worse, want was widespread, affecting not only Armenians. The vali issued orders that each were to look after one's own poor—Armenian helping Armenian, Turk helping Turk, Kurd helping Kurd. KBF hoped that "Dr. Kimball will not have as much trouble now." But enforcing the edict would be difficult, if not impossible. Given their status as less than Turk or Kurd, the Armenians would be the first to be forced to give up whatever they had.

Amidst the violence, loss, and suffering, KBF wrote of some events that warmed her heart and provided hope that generosity and love still existed. A bright and promising young woman, Satinug Dodregian, notified KBF that her family could not pay her school fees for the term. Although KBF told her she could continue at the school regardless of her family's ability to pay, Satinug declined the charity. Much to KBF's delight, three young women whom she identifies as Anna Der Harostoorian, Markrooke Nalpandian, and Mariam Mahesian contributed five piastres each to cover the bill. Anna also contributed "a suit of clothing" for Satinug to wear to school. KBF noted that prior to this act of generosity, Mariam spent considerable time knitting thick, warm socks for another child from a poor family who attended the school tuition-free and whose clothes came from items donated to the mission.

In spring 1894, the Armenians came down from their hiding places, ready to fight for their rights. Unfair taxation and the theft of about two hundred sheep by migrating Kurds led to more fighting. By August, Sultan Abdul Hamid II sent his own troops to suppress what he claimed was an Armenian rebellion. Together, the soldiers and the Kurds attacked and burned villages, raped women, and murdered an estimated three thousand people without regard for age or sex.

Reports by British officials in the region caused an international outcry, leading Sultan Abdul Hamid II to downplay the number killed and lay blame at the feet of the Kurds, painting them as uncontrollable barbarians. Further, a commission established by the Sultan to investigate the massacre found the Armenians at fault for not wanting to pay taxes. The British consul, however, knew of one eyewitness account of representatives from one Armenian village presenting proof they had paid their taxes. The official to whom they presented the receipts ignored the evidence and ordered the village surrounded and all inhabitants put to death.

The shockwaves felt by the international community were even greater close to the ground zero of events. KBF and her associates in Van went about their business and reassured students at the school that all would be well. Her letters home are light in tone and give no indication of the massacres. She wrote little about them in her journal, but one entry provides a hint that some Armenians felt they could not trust even the mission's doctors. KBF recorded that Dr. Kimball was "all broken up" after a dying patient's family questioned whether she provided him with adequate care.

On December 17, 1894, KBF wrote to someone named Sam. While her letters throughout the year had avoided details of the events of the summer, in this one, she decided "I am going to tell you about the awful affair which happened in the Sansoon region. We have not considered it safe to speak about it hitherto and indeed this letter may never reach you." This is the first of several letters in which KBF evoked the image of Tamburlaine, the theatrical character synonymous with harshness, violence, and savagery.

> The firman [the Sultan's decree of reforms] was read and everyone declared disloyal to the Sultan and Islam who spared man, woman, or child....
>
> The carnage began. The Kurds were pushed to the front and the Armenians fought for their lives but it was simply a wholesale butchering. The Kurds were inclined to spare women and children, but the soldiers killed them off.
>
> From the circumference of the region they worked in toward the centre, as huntsmen surround their game, and every village was a scene of murder, rape, and plunder. This continued for sixteen or twenty days, the most brutal work being done on the 29th of August, the Sultan's birthday, near Tadoorg, where the Armenians had gathered to make their last stand. No pleading for quarter, no protestation of innocence or plea for women and children met with anything but torture and death. The troops were not withdrawn until the work was thoroughly finished.
>
> Ninety miles of prosperous region was converted into a desert. Crops were destroyed and the flocks and herds were divided among the troops and Kurds.
>
> Thirty two, some say forty villages were destroyed and the victims numbered from twenty to thirty thousand. Mr. Hallward, to make his report believable, put the number at 5000.

> I could tell you stories of horror that would tax the imagination. Tamourlane never did worse things I am sure. It made me sick to my soul to hear of them and I could not sleep that night after first hearing of the awful atrocities committed.

The world in which she found herself was so foreign to her life back in North America. Memories of family and community in Nova Scotia must have felt so far away, and not just in terms of physical distance. Connection through correspondence was essential, and this comes through in the letter from which the preceding excerpt was taken. Just before she signed off, she added: “And, by and by, when you can spare a little time, don’t you want to write me one of your nice, helpful letters? So many of my friends have stopped writing regularly to me that I sometimes feel a wee bit forgotten.”

Chapter Six

"We held our breath as the horses went slipping along"

Between 1894 and 1896, KBF's journal entries and correspondence vacillate between disbelief of deteriorating conditions and hopelessness upon learning that they are true. Not surprisingly, her health suffers. She endures frequent headaches, which she attributes to malaria, feels tired and short-tempered, experiences muddled thinking, and finds herself in tears at minor provocations and inconveniences, symptoms that could be attributed to the ingestion over time of strychnine and arsenic in the pills Dr. Smith prescribed her to take daily. In several letters, she put on a brave face, telling her sisters that she was confident in God's benevolence and protection. Though that faith never wavered, it was frequently tested.

July 1894 brought a strong, reassuring presence for the mission staff in the person of the new British vice consul. KBF gave the following description of Cecil M. Hallward: "very tall, six feet two inches, good form and rather good looking...a good clear complexion, very fair and is fine looking. He is immensely dignified quite enough as for a man of forty instead of one who is only thirty one. We have the deepest respect for him and the people almost worship him, as well they should." Months later, she would write her sister: "We all felt that under God he has been the means of keeping peace in Van this winter. We think if it had not been for his presence there would undoubtedly have been a massacre. He is odd, according to our opinion, in some ways, but since I have ridden so much with him, I think perhaps the oddity was on our side."

In September 1894, conditions were sufficiently stable that KBF planned a trip to Oroomiah, Persia (Urmia, Iran) for a meeting of missionaries. The distance between Van and Urmia is about three hundred kilometres, easily traversed in a day in modern vehicles. But in the late nineteenth century, the journey through the region took five or six days, so was not undertaken on a light-hearted whim for adventure.

Initially KBF planned to travel on her own as part of a caravan (an indicator of how relatively safe she felt), then meet up with a missionary by the name of Mr. Mecklin three days later in Salmas, Persia. Together, they planned to travel to Hamadan, the capital of the Persian province of the same name. When Reverend Herbert Allen of the Van mission offered to accompany her for the first three days, she accepted readily, grateful to travel in the company of one whom she knew.

The first night of the journey, KBF and Mr. Allen pitched tents in a small Armenian village. When they set out the following day, they left the tents behind because they were cumbersome, believing they would find further accommodations in the villages ahead. The village they reached before nightfall, however, was so poor that nothing could be found and they set up camp beds beneath the stars. KBF wrote that although the night air was "slightly cool," a "glorious canopy" of stars more than distracted her from any small discomfort. "I never saw a more beautiful starlight night. It was almost twelve when we finally got settled and at that time of night in September, some of the first constellations are to be seen Perseus, Orion, Taurus.... I felt very safe and contented and finally, with Jupiter shining directly over my head with the calm feeling in my heart that the One who has created the Heavens and hung it in such wonderful lights to lighten the world for His creation would keep in safety one of His little ones sleeping in a lonely mountain village, I fell asleep."

They set out on the third morning with a zaptieh to escort them. Some new Kurdish guides also joined the caravan, one of whom particularly impressed her. "[Y]ou should have seen the handsome Kurd they gave us. Costume, large shalvas (pants), blue stripe, red broadcloth jacket, short and open like Eton jacket showing a gorgeous coloured shirt, long sleeves...beautiful embroidery, and a girdle of silk filled with cartridges, the usual cartridge belt not on, and a Persian scarf tied around his fez in the jauntiest way possible. He was really the handsomest Kurd I've seen and very nice, too."

The day passed uneventfully, but upon reaching the gates of the vank where they expected to meet Mr. Mecklin, "out rushed two Persian Kurds, and I thought they were going to take possession of me and run off at once." After some confusion, during which KBF described herself as "rattled" particularly because the Kurds focused on her and ignored both Rev. Allen and the zaptieh, who did nothing, one of the Kurds produced a letter from Mr. Mecklin, telling her he was detained and directing KBF to permit the two Kurds to escort her into Persia. KBF knew that Rev. Allen wished to return to Van as soon as possible because every male normally at the mission was away on other business, leaving the women and children alone. "So I told him—Mr. Allen—that I would go along with [the Kurds] the next day.... They swore before God they would take me safely to [Salmas]."

Once inside the vank, however, the head priest cautioned them "to not believe a word the Kurds told us, that the road to [Salmas] was an exceedingly dangerous one. The Kurds on the border were fighting among themselves and killing each other." After listening to some "blood curdling" tales, they consulted a Turkish official who corroborated the priest's stories and "said it would not do at all for me to go alone." Rev. Allen reluctantly agreed to continue the journey with her.

They continued their journey the following morning, initially without incident. Shortly after midday, however, one of their Kurdish escorts halted near some ruins, insisting he "saw two mounted men prowling behind." The other Kurd told KBF and Rev. Allen that the first was lying in order to frighten them. They halted nonetheless and the first Kurd went to a village nearby. After an absence during which they wondered whether he would return, he came back in an agitated state. He informed them of an altercation between Kurdish tribesmen and Persian soldiers the night before, during which one of the soldiers died. Because both Kurdish escorts belonged to the tribe engaged in the fighting, they refused to venture any further, fearing imprisonment if they went to Salmas.

The Kurdish guides demanded the fee negotiated at the beginning of the trip. KBF observed the situation would have been "[a] nice little dilemma for me had I been alone" because she carried no cash, knowing the guides were to be paid by Mr. Mecklin once they reached their destination. Though they questioned the veracity of the Kurds' claim of imminent arrest, they were in no position to argue. Rev. Allen negotiated with their guides to pay them if they took them as close as possible to Salmas. They agreed, taking them to within two hours of the city. KBF and Rev. Allen completed that part of the journey on their own, arriving in Salmas without incident, where they met Mr. Mecklin who confirmed that the Kurds' story about fighting was true.

Rev. Allen left KBF in the company of Mr. Mecklin and a Dr. Wright to continue on to Urmia and began his journey back to Van. KBF's party stopped for the night in Gavlan, in what is now West Azerbaijan Province in Iran. There they joined several others also heading to Urmia.

KBF gave no indication in her letters how long she stayed in Urmia. She enjoyed the city, which, though beautiful, she found not as attractive as Van for "natural beauty." She described reaching the grounds of the Christian college there and thinking "we had reached America instead. The well cared for grounds, with an abundant water supply, the stately trees, the large brick building and neat cottages seemed altogether too much like civilization to find in an eastern city."

Though her surviving letters do not describe her activities or list those whom she met while there, her surviving Psalmist gives clues to at least some of her activity. In its pages, she pasted copies of letters describing some of her experiences and the massacres and their aftermath. Among her papers are copies of newspaper articles containing this same information, including one article attributed to "Miss Kate B. Fraser" and another to "A Nova Scotia Lady Missionary." None of the others mention her or feature bylines, but the wording of articles are verbatim from the notes pasted in her Psalmist.

If KBF found aspects of the trip to Urmia unsettling, the return journey to Van brought one that terrified her. Her party set out on a Monday morning later than anticipated, escorted by three Kurdish guides. "Everything went beautifully all day but in the evening before the stars came out in all their beauty, it began to grow a little weird as we journeyed along, no one speaking and only the clatter of horses' hoofs on the stones to break the stillness of the night."

The travellers reached a pass, where they encountered "a bad piece of road, where we seemed shut in even from Heaven and we held our breath as the horses went slipping along." KBF felt relief on reaching the other side of the pass. She brought her horse alongside that of her colleague and friend, an American teacher at the mission, Elizabeth Huntingdon, with whom she began to chat. Suddenly, all the horses "with one accord stood perfectly still and almost immediately a bullet went whizzing by our ears, followed in quick succession by others." They scrambled for cover as their guides returned fire and the men in the party drew out rifles and side arms to assist in repelling the attack. One of the men told the women to run, but the Kurds shouted at them to go slow. "We considered it the wisest part of valour to go slow or stand still."

The mission party took cover, and after a further exchange of gunfire, the attackers retreated. Only then did KBF feel the small trickle of blood on the side of her face. On closer inspection, she found that a bullet had carried off a lock of hair, grazing her ear in the process. One can imagine her gratitude upon reaching the vank an hour later, "very thankful indeed for the protection which had been granted us [by] these strong Kurd[ish escorts]."

Despite the constant threat of violence, KBF seemed to prefer it to quiet domesticity. In a letter to Sadie, written a few months before the incident travelling from Urmia, KBF wondered if Tina would be angry if KBF shared a secret with Sadie: that a Methodist minister by the name of Munro who visited Sherbrooke the previous summer had fallen in love with Tina and proposed to her with a wish to be married in June; thus far Tina had not given him an answer. As excited as she was for her sister, knowing "it would be a pity to have two old maids in the family," KBF was less enthusiastic about her domestic prospects should her sister marry. "I am wondering if I have to go home in the summer, shall I have Grace enough to settle down and be my Father's housekeeper?" As difficult as KBF's early experiences as a missionary had been, "it resulted in a more real happiness than I ever enjoyed. It will take more Grace than I shall be able to command in months to be willing to be a home missionary, but I really am striving very hard with the flesh.... You will find me very humble and ready to be good. Tina has really had her share and if the Methodist parson is nice...I ought to be willing to take my turn at staying home."

For a full year before Red Cross relief teams would get permission to land in Turkey in the spring of 1896, missionaries carried out what relief work they could. In June 1895, Grace Kimball wrote to her colleague and mentor at Vassar, Dr. Elizabeth Theldberg, that with twenty dollars cash she had on hand, she created an "industrial bureau" by purchasing wool and cotton to distribute to local women to card and spin. Those materials became socks, garments, and rugs to sell and to distribute to refugees. Kimball reported that within a few months, sixteen thousand people earned wages in the cotton, wool, and garment factories and in the six bakeries she established.

KBF's surviving letters for 1895 frequently express impatience and ill-temper, most likely caused by the stress of the huge demands, which they could not hope to meet, to alleviate the suffering around them. She began one to her sisters in early July 1895 as follows:

> The mail came in this morning but it wasn't very much of a one. There was no home letter. I suspect some of my letters go astray, too, or do you get one each week from me? I invariably write although sometimes I don't put enough on my epistles to be worth a postage stamp. That will be the case probably with this. I have had a hard day and I think perhaps I am nearly cross. Anyway, I am not in a good humor for talking with my friends, but as the post will not delay its out going until I get good natured again, I fulfill my duty to write now.

Another written to her sister a few weeks later begins on an even more tart note. Even though she was tired and wanted to go to bed, she wrote the letter, knowing she wouldn't have a minute to write the next day "and as I have not missed a week yet in sending my home letter, I do not wish to begin to grow careless at the entrance of my fourth year." Her sister couldn't have failed to catch the bitter reproach. If KBF could find time to write during hellish times, then surely her sister could take some time from her comparatively easy life.

The end of July 1895 brought some slight respite, as the mission staff journeyed up Mount Varag, where they set up camp "between two peaks which shuts us in and gives us late mornings and early evenings." There she enjoyed the cool mountain air, which reminded her more of October than mid-summer. The fresh air gave her an appetite and at one point she complained that tea time meant just that—"simply tea, not the meal we speak of as tea at home."

Still expected to give lessons, she was delighted when one day Mr. Allen suggested that instead of her descending to Van, her boys would enjoy a day's excursion to her. After attending an early chapel service, the boys hiked up to the camp, where they "adjourned to the little knoll by the side of our brook and had a nice little class." Afterwards, the boys were given a meal of "native bread and eggs cooked as they like them," because the return journey would see them arrive home very late. "The rest of the day I have been lazing in the hammock, sometimes reading 'The Roses of the Old Testament' and sometimes sleeping. My boys told me I had already begun to get fat. Oh, it is so delightful to bask in the sunshine a whole day at a time."

One day, KBF, Dr. Raynolds, and Elizabeth Huntingdon set out with servants and donkeys to hike to the top of Mount Varag—at 3,200 metres, reaching the peak was not an easy undertaking; the slopes were steep and covered in loose rocks. Halfway up, Elizabeth Huntingdon and the servants asked to stop. Dr. Raynolds and KBF continued to the summit from which Huntingdon and the servants "looked like Liliputians in the distance... [The] view was simply sublime, impossible to describe.... He told Mrs. Reynolds [*sic*] when we got back that his hair stood on end to see me climbing up the steep rocks.... Well, I've been over 11,000 feet up in the air. I may go higher some day but certainly I don't want to go up Varank again."

Rested and refreshed, the party was ready to return to their work and the start of another school year. In her journal, KBF recorded on September 2 that she "had such a good time during the four weeks spent [in the mountains]." But by September 12, the summer respite was a distant memory: "School began Monday. 9 o'clock brought the children & a good many mothers to beg that their daughters should be rec'd free or at less than the usual price. Tiresome & nervous work to talk with them. Satinug down in the kindergarten with Miss Huntingdon leaves one short upstairs. Baron Levonian's lessons to be arranged for. Troubles on all sides because Armina & Hamas are still in Erzeroum. Time tables, arranging classes, changing books, etc., has been the order of the week. Having not been very well the work has seemed heavy."

Short-staffed and with the uncertainty whether funds would come in to continue their work, KBF wrote that the kindergarten teacher, Satinug, "has been down in the dumps and almost saucy." To her journal KBF confided: "The result of her tantrums & perhaps too much standing on my feet when not feeling well has been a fit of the blues & a good cry. I believe the 'good cry' has done me good. Anyway I feel much braver & ready to take up the battle again tomorrow. Oh, for more wisdom & power to do things as they should be done."

In mid-September, KBF wrote to her sister, who had recently become Mrs. Tina Munro:

> You will be interested in our new boarder, a little girl whom we took in last week. Last Sunday/Monday morning, Zozo came to me and asked me to allow a little girl to whom we had been giving bread for some time, to come to school and learn how to read. I asked her history and we talked the matter over together and decided to take her in and keep her as a boarder. Her father and mother died when she was a baby and her uncle cared for her until a short time ago when either not caring to keep her any longer or not being able to, he took her out on the mountainside and left her exposed. Some Kurds found her wandering about and brought her to Van. She was left at the house of one of our own school boys who is very poor. He took her around begging for several days and that is the way we began giving her bread. She is a bright little thing and I wish you could see her today, such a difference in the little thing. We have had an entire outfit made for her.

> She was almost naked last Sunday morning and her little feet were bruised and swollen, her eyes very sore. But now they are quite well and she looks well cared for and happy.
>
> When Hosep brought her things from the bazaar, I had her come to try on her shoes. They were miles too big, of course, and had to be changed. She understood she couldn't have a pair and when she got almost out of sight began crying. I called her back and showed her the material for her outfit and had one of the children explain that another pair of shoes would be forthcoming. She grew radiant again and has been as happy as possible ever since this morning [when she] was dressed entirely for the first time and when I went into say good morning to the girls I scarcely recognised the little child that came up to kiss my hand as a token of thankfulness.

In a letter to her sisters at the end of September, it seems as though the summer break had never happened.

> Dr. Kimball's work is growing and the need is also terribly increasing. The English Friends have been helping and indeed are continuing their efforts to help along the work but we need more help. Do you think it possible to collect any money at home for the poor starving people? I know were the hardest hearted person in Sherbrooke to see a group of these ragged and starving people he would at once put his hand in his pocket and give something. I am going to send a plea to Yarmouth and see if the people there will not help us. With the cool weather coming on the want is

> pressing. If you should succeed in getting any money send it to Miss May, Congregational House, Somerset St. Boston and she will send it to me.
>
> A woman has just this minute been in begging for wool to spin. She begs help in God's name, tells me she will kiss my feet if I'll only ask Dr. K. to give her work. I tell her I will intercede for her tomorrow as today Dr. K is not giving out work and with a God Bless you she goes out. I do not see how Dr. Kimball stands the strain as she does. The few people who come to me break me all up and she sees hundreds of them. It has been telling on her tho', and last week we were afraid she would have to give in for a while. This week she is quite herself again.

News reached the mission early in October 1895 of a violent clash between Armenians and the police on September 30 in Constantinople. Members of the Hunchak Party demonstrated to demand reforms suggested earlier in the summer by Great Britain, France, and Russia to control the Kurds and to employ Christian assistant governors throughout Turkish districts, in the hope of maintaining peace. In the aftermath of the demonstration in Constantinople, massacres spread throughout the country. "Then we have heard that torpedoes are being laid in the Bosphorous which indicates war, and my dear it may break upon us at any time," KBF reported to her sister. Even so, KBF assured her they would "pray to have such an evil averted, and I scarcely think we shall have to fly the country yet awhile." In fact, KBF's prediction proved accurate. They remained in Van for almost a year. KBF added to her letter: "Perhaps it would be just as well for you not to say anything about a probable war to the others yet."

A new vali replaced his predecessor in October 1895. KBF and her colleagues found him fierce-looking but genial, giving them high hopes that between him and the efforts of the British vice consul, they would be kept safe from harm. Even so, there was talk among mission members that "the ladies of the station [should go] to Persia." KBF's opinion was that to do so "would be like flying from one possible danger into a positive one for the roads are fearfully dangerous." Doubtless she recalled being shot at. Besides, Mr. Hallward assured them they "would be safe" at the mission station because "the [Turkish] government has special orders in reference to Europeans."

Grace Knapp, the daughter of missionaries George and Elizabeth Knapp whom KBF met in Bitlis during her first year in Turkey, arrived at the mission on October 5, 1895, for "three or four weeks" on vacation to "get ready for her winter's work" back in Bitlis. According to KBF, she "is young, very quiet, and I fear somewhat hard to entertain. Perhaps she will not allow me to realize my fears, tho'." Of course, entertainment was the least of their worries in light of the increasing threat of violence and massacre.

KBF's journal entry for October 23, 1895, is a single line: "Rumour of massacre [in Bitlis]." Grace Knapp's father was in charge of the mission there.

A few days later, KBF wrote her cousin Sadie in Princeton:

> The air is dark and sad, and the clouds are gathering blackly above us. Such is the aspect of nature today and such is the aspect that the political situation is assuming. You know that for several months there has been danger of an outbreak [of violence] and we have often gone to bed with rumors of massacres ringing in our ears. Since last Monday there has been a little more

talk. Both Turks and Armenians are armed, the latter having been secretly importing rifles and ammunition for some time.

On Wednesday some soldiers arrived from outlying villages and immediately the report was circulated that they had come in to help massacre the Christians. Many Armenians closed their stores and hurried home. Everyone was alarmed and not knowing whether the Christians would try to subdue their hotheaded friends. We felt that there was a good deal of danger. A single impudent word or act just now would mean perhaps a great deal of bloodshed.

However, Thursday morning everything was quiet and I rode into the city as usual on that day. On my way I saw more rifles and cartridge belts than I had seen in a long time, but otherwise there was no sign of disturbance. Our teachers of the city school were greatly reassured when they saw me. They had been too frightened to go to bed the night before but they decided that if it were safe for me to come to them, they were all right.

Yesterday morning we were compelled to listen to wild rumours and I fear this time there is truth in them. Word comes that there has been a massacre in Bitlis and Moosh. Indeed, when the telegram arrived fighting was still going on. We are much alarmed for the safety of our friends there but we shall wait in hope until tomorrow morning. It is true that there has been a disturbance in Bitlis but of how serious a nature we do not know. All day yesterday the guards patrolled the streets to keep the peace. Armenians flocked home from the bazaars and the Turks buckled on their armor

> for they are as afraid of the Armenians as the latter are of them.
>
> Our boarders heard the rumour about noon yesterday and [one of the Armenian teachers] rushed to my room to ask about it and to take me to pacify the children who were all crying and screaming with fear. Poor little wretches. I felt so sorry for them. It did not take very long to get them to listen to reason, but the fact that I was going riding with Mr. Hallward a little later was more reassuring than anything I could say. They knew if there was immediate danger I would not go.

Rev. Allen, however, believed it was not safe to venture out. He agreed reluctantly when she assured him that she would be in the company of Mr. Hallward, and he cautioned them both to return before dark. She assured Rev. Allen that it was her habit to return before dark, as it "doesn't do to be out after sunset in the malarious air."

But they didn't return before dark. Mr. Hallward suggested a trip through side streets to see "whether the population seemed much excited." They found the streets almost deserted, "but the very silence seemed portentous, the air seemed to quiver with danger." KBF was so thoroughly unnerved by the time they returned to the mission compound that she could not eat her supper. To add to her anxiety, Grace Kimball visited KBF's room that evening "more disturbed...than she has been yet." Missionaries at Bitlis managed to cable the ominous message: "We still live." They discussed the message with Rev. Allen, and all agreed that any news should be kept, as long as humanly possible, from Grace Knapp. They told her she had to remain in Van because the road to Bitlis was too dangerous to travel, even with an armed escort.

Turkish police deserted their guard houses in the Armenian district to gather in the Turkish quarter. Armenians gathered in churches, "evidently ready, if reason should be given, to defend themselves." The head of the Armenian Church sent word to the vali that he would "keep the Armenians quiet" in exchange for which the vali pledged to "be responsible for the Turks." KBF felt that, had the old vali still been in charge, violence would have already broken out.

Tense days passed and evenings brought the chance to "breathe easier" in the belief that any attacks would happen in broad daylight. News continued to trickle in about violence and precarious peace in other communities. They telegraphed George Knapp in Bitlis to enquire about conditions there and were alarmed to receive no response. But nothing could be done. They could only wait.

The tone of a letter from KBF to her sister around this time is slightly different to that of the one she wrote to her cousin. Perhaps the distance between Sadie's home in Princeton and KBF's family in Sherbrooke enabled KBF to be more open in her letters to Sadie. Or perhaps Sadie's friends and contacts had a better idea of what was happening in Turkey, and KBF didn't feel such a need to downplay the rapidly disintegrating situation in Van.

KBF's letter of October 29, 1895, to her sister not only downplays but dismisses the very threat she described to Sadie two days before. "Today as far as I have heard there is perfect peace" in Van. She rode out to Lake Van with Mr. Hallward, where "the air along the lakeshore is so delightful. I wish you could have been along." Her journal confirms that she did, indeed, ride out with Mr. Hallward.

The vali, whom KBF described here and elsewhere as "a very sensible man," reassured them that peace would be maintained. When Rev. Allen asked for an armed escort, the vali "was perfectly willing to give it" but convinced Rev. Allen to forego it, as it might give people the wrong impression and lead some to attack, rather than maintain order.

KBF ended the letter saying that by the time the letter reached her sister, doubtless "everything will have quieted down. I feel that it will be so or I would not tell you about it, as we have had rumours of massacres all winter and I haven't thought it worth while dwelling too much on them." And even if the worst happened, she was confident "we would receive the protection of the government."

She added a postscript to the letter, answering a reference by her sister to an article written by Mr. William Willard Howard of the Reuters news agency and reassuring her that things weren't as bad as he painted them. "Tell Father not to worry. If anything should happen I'll telegraph. I haven't missed my daily rides so you know it isn't as bad as it might be. That article of Mr. Howard's will cause a sensation.... But my dear nothing will happen to us unless it is our Father's will, and so we feel safe."

Increasing pressure by Western governments led the Sultan to issue a firman, or decree of reforms, in late October 1895, though doing so seemed only to confirm his suspicion that the Armenians posed a threat to his government. By the time he issued the firman, there was little hope or belief that any reforms would be adopted. At the beginning of November, KBF wrote, "Now for the enforcement of them, reforms on paper being worse than useless." At the end of the month she wrote again of the "useless, yea worse than useless Bill of Reform," convinced that the Sultan's plan was "to put an end to the Christians as soon as possible & in the most inhuman way possible."

Nerves frayed as tensions mounted. In early November, KBF wrote in her journal that, though "peace still reigns in Van...across the lake...[the] Kurds have devastated thirty villages, literally leaving the poor villagers homeless, naked & starving." The only consolation was that "this time, the Kurds were content to plunder without taking life." A bit further along she wrote:

> Yesterday's mail was far from being a cheerful one. It brought us word of a bad outbreak in Erzeroum. The consul wrote to Mr. H. that the number of killed would certainly be in at least three figures. He wrote the day of the trouble & had not learned the details. There was no letter from Bitlis & we still are anxious for our friends there. The extent of the massacre there is not known. Trebizond's number 5 or 600. Van seems to be the safest city in Turkey at present but the citizens have been in great fear for several weeks. Perhaps the missionaries also?

The efforts of Kimball and her colleagues, promoted by friends in the US and through the publication of some of their letters home, garnered more financial support in November 1895 with donations of $500 from the *Christian Herald* and of $500, then $5,000 from Dr. Thomas De Witt Talmage, editor of the *Herald*, cabled via an entity called the Bible House Committee, based in Constantinople. The *Herald* hired Mr. William Willard Howard of the Reuters news agency to deliver to Kimball a further $10,000 raised by the newspaper. But as it turned out, Howard only made it as far as Ooromiah, Persia (Urmia, Iran), home to numerous missions established by

Catholic and Anglican churches from the US and Great Britain.

Louis Klopsch had purchased the *Christian Herald* in 1889, installing Talmage as its editor. Under Klopsch's guidance, subscriptions skyrocketed. Together, Klopsch and Talmage endeavoured to make the weekly paper a mouthpiece and conduit to create the leading Christian international relief organization in the United States. Initially, the goal to provide relief regardless of religion or nationality was a success. But when the *Herald* provided relief to earthquake victims in Turkey in 1894, one letter changed the organization's direction. A subscriber wanted to know why relief dollars were being directed to both Muslims and Christians in a country that did not treat its Christian minority with equality. Though Klopsch, an immigrant himself, tried to plead that all those who suffered deserved help, his subscribers were solidly grounded in evangelical Christianity. In order to placate its base, the *Herald* determined to concentrate only on aid "which resonated with American ideals of religious liberty"—which, in effect, meant deserving Christians.

The newspaper spared no details in reporting vicious attacks by Muslims against Christians, portraying Turks as diabolical and savage, and pleading that the paper could not provide greater details (though there were plenty) at the risk of offending readers' delicate sensibilities. Money poured in, and the *Herald* became the major conduit for foreign aid in the US. But their popular and inflammatory articles had a negative impact. Evangelical Christians weren't the only ones reading the *Herald*.

Aware of articles Howard penned for American papers about what he knew of Armenian suffering based on his own travels in Turkey a year earlier, in 1894, the Turkish government refused him entry to the country. While Howard was en route to Turkey, the US State Department cautioned Klopsch that this might happen. Howard waited in Persia, making several appeals to Turkish officials to let him in. They refused each time. The following year, 1896, Howard published a book entitled *Horrors of Armenia: The Story of an Eye-witness*. Comparing Howard's book with KBF's letters in which she describes her personal experiences and exchanges with Grace Kimball, it becomes clear that his book—in which Howard claims he "speaks from knowledge acquired by nearly a year and a half of personal observation and careful investigation in the distressed country"—actually contains information acquired from his correspondence with these two women.

In several letters home, KBF expressed disappointment that Turkey barred Mr. Howard's entry. Grace Kimball's response was more measured. She bore complete responsibility for the work in which she and her colleagues engaged. She enjoyed good relations with the new vali. Kimball and her colleagues visited his household regularly, making gifts of produce from the mission's gardens. The vali, in turn, gifted them with trout "from the Lignis," which were "very rare in Van" according to one of KBF's letters. Mission members visited the vali's home; women from the mission socialized with his wives and family.

Kimball knew that, to a certain degree, they continued their relief work because of these good relations. She wrote in November 1895 that Howard's inability to enter Turkey might be something of a blessing. "[T]here is some fear lest his presence [in Van] should turn the suspicions of the government toward this work, and thus defeat the whole thing.... You can easily see that when it is the deliberate policy of the [Sublime] Porte [the central government of the Ottoman Empire] to blot out its Christian subjects, our work, unless done quietly, will be apt to meet with opposition in some indirect but effective manner. I have had my industrial bureau working now nearly six months, and whatever I may do in a quiet way towards enlarging it and adding other agencies is not so likely to attract attention as to have a stranger come in." For the time being, the funds cabled via the Bible House Committee were sufficient to keep them going.

In a letter to the *Christian Herald* dated November 25, 1895, Kimball wrote that she felt that her "position in relation to the Christian Herald fund is somewhat delicate, but common sense and the exigencies of the case leads me to act as your self-constituted agent until such time as Mr. Howard arrives." Kimball also acted as "the executive agent for the English Women's Armenian Relief Fund, with the British Vice-Consul C. M. Hallward, as auditor." On that basis, she reported that funds helped them to distribute over five hundred pounds of bread. "My modus operandi is to have registered families according to the villages, making record of the amount of property of which they were robbed, how many killed and wounded, if any, etc. Then they are passed over to me and I supply them with clothing from the product of the Industrial Bureau and give them a ticket for the proper amount of bread to be had daily at the bakery."

KBF assisted in the administration of relief services and would eventually copy Kimball's model for organization when she was charged, in the autumn of 1896, with organizing thousands of Armenian refugees in Varna, Bulgaria.

Chapter Seven

"A reign of terror"

Van was one of the last communities to feel the full effects of massacres that laid waste to towns and villages. News in the form of letters and telegrams reached the mission in Van on a weekly basis. Members counted on the good graces of the vali and the diplomacy of the British, French, and Russian governments with the Sultan to ensure they could carry on their work safely. The increase in activities by revolutionary and other dissident groups, including armed clashes with police and soldiers, brought unwanted focus on Christian missionaries. As far as the Sultan was concerned, what was to say that these groups weren't sympathetic to the dissidents? Perhaps they fomented unrest, if not actively, then by their very presence in communities all over Turkey.

To complicate matters, neighbours began to view neighbours with suspicion. So-called "Turkophiles" in the Armenian communities—those who believed in appease-ment or who shared genuine friendships with their Turkish

There is a long history of Armenian women fighting to defend their communities. This picture was taken in 1895; little is known about these two women. (SOURCE UNKNOWN)

neighbours—were deemed a threat. Armenian community leaders and church elders suffered attacks, and sometimes death, raising suspicion to levels almost as paranoid as those of Sultan Abdul Hamid II. Some accused Turks of the attacks and claimed they laid the blame at Armenian feet in order to fracture relationships within the community. Others credited loyal Armenians of eliminating their disloyal brothers. And, as has been the case almost throughout human history, there were divisions along age lines, with most elders urging passive acceptance of their lot in life, and many young people angrily rejecting their treatment as second-class citizens. Those who lived many years under Turkish rule saw no other way. Others were young enough to see other possibilities and were willing to fight—die, if necessary—in order to gain them.

The community in Van was no exception, with most elders urging calm when young people declared a desire to take up arms. KBF frequently expressed impatience with the Revolutionists, believing that their increasing stockpile of weapons would invite a massacre by the Turks, killing them all. Against the tense backdrop, the mission continued its work, planting gardens, tending to the sick, and educating the youth. Letters home describe domestic life, but increasingly there are references to outbreaks of unrest and violence, and of such events increasingly coming closer to Van.

KBF wrote to Sadie on November 3, 1895, that Dr. Raynolds's wife, Martha, "suffered more than anyone else these last few weeks...[and] is in a perfect state of worry all the time." KBF admitted there was some substance to the stories that caused Mrs. Raynolds such distress. "The Koords [*sic*] are getting beyond all control in the villages around us.... Thursday a man came to us who had been branded from thigh to foot by two Koords because he refused to do some little thing for them. His leg was in a perfectly awful condition.... The sight made me sick to the very soul." In her journal she wrote of reports that some "parents buried some of their larger girls in the sand leaving only a small breathing hole, to keep them safe from the Kurds." With stories and sights such as this, it is little wonder Mrs. Raynolds felt nervous. But Martha Raynolds was made of sterner stuff. Though she would leave Van with the mission's wives and children in the spring of 1896, she eventually returned there, remaining with her husband until her death in Tiflis during the evacuation of Van at the height of the genocide in 1915.

The government dispatched troops throughout the country, allegedly to keep peace. KBF was either unaware, or didn't believe the general opinion among Armenians and missionaries alike, that, though purportedly sent to keep the Kurds in line, Turkish troops' public orders to the Kurds were countered in private meetings during which Kurdish leaders were given license to kill. KBF could hardly believe the truth when she learned it. "Fancy government troops acting in such a diabolical manner!"

KBF's previous desire to soften things for her sisters began to slip in late November. Referring to an article by a Mr. Dillon in an English publication called *The Contemporary Review*, KBF writes, "It is the most awful thing I ever read, awful because I know his statements are only too true. How can the people of Christian Europe and Russia read such an article without wishing to rise in their might and crush out the power that causes so much misery? This is no political question that is causing so much trouble. It is a war of the cross and the Christian world will some day awake to this fact."

Without reading the article, some might wonder whether Mr. Dillon sought to fan the flames. Turkey, after all, was a Muslim nation. There was concern that Western governments wished to topple Turkey's Muslim government, replacing it with a Christian government and making Muslims if not a minority, then certainly the oppressed. Such is the nature of rhetoric, which, while it has some basis in the "truth" of a particular group or groups, whips up fear by playing on emotion. We witnessed a similar, though inverted, example in 2016 during the UK's campaign to leave the European Union—"Brexit"—when advocates of "Leave" preyed upon concerns of British voters that Turkey would gain membership in the European Union. Disregarding the fact that any one member of the EU—Britain, had it decided to remain—had the power to veto such membership, many at the time cited this prospective membership as their primary reason for voting to leave the European Union.

Word finally reached the Van compound in early November 1895 that, although locked down, the mission in Bitlis was intact. The missionaries reported the deaths of Armenians but weren't certain of numbers. The vali of Bitlis took the mission there under his auspices to protect its occupants from attack, sending nineteen zaptiehs to guard it in early December. Given the suspicion that George Knapp not only sympathized with the Revolutionists but advocated their attacks upon the Kurds, the vali might also have wished to keep an eye on Knapp and his colleagues, preventing them from circulating easily in the community.

KBF confided to her journal on November 11, 1895,

> Everyone blue tonight. At the Allens, Mr. Hallward, Dr. K. & Mr. A are discussing the advisability of sending the ladies of the station over to Persia. I hope it will not be decided to send us. Such a decision makes one feel that the danger is very near. For a while I believe I was nervous. The girls could not understand my tendency to laugh at every trivial saying this evening but they were reassured by my apparent lightheartedness that the rumors of the massacre had no foundation. Dear girls. I wanted to cry for them & the only way to keep from doing so was to laugh.

In late November, KBF wrote again to her cousin Sadie in Princeton, describing the previous three weeks as "a reign of terror" with "the most diabolical work right around us." "All the villages in our near vicinity have been first plundered & then destroyed, the people have fled to the city naked & starving. All last week they kept pouring in. How your heart would have ached could you have seen the ragged & forlorn creatures surging past our doors. At the present moment our yard is full of women & children crying for clothing & something to eat."

Bazaars, schools, and businesses closed. People living on the periphery of Aikesdan, The Garden City, moved closer to the centre of Van, fearing their positions made them vulnerable to attack. Rev. Allen assured his colleagues that they stood ready to repel any attack with "460 shots and lots of ammunition to load up again." Both Turks and Armenians were heavily armed, which, though failing to create a détente, certainly helped to keep both sides in check for the time being while "everyone waits for the sword to fall." The situation was less reassuring for their colleagues in Bitlis. "Our friends in Bitlis have been & are in terrible danger. They are living with barricaded doors, windows filled with flagstones & tables piled with arms ready to defend themselves. Mr. Knapp does not dare show himself outside & he had not taken his clothes off for 15 days when we last heard. As soon as a strong escort can be provided they are all coming to us. The killed there have numbered probably 500. In Erzeroum Mr. Chambers writes 'the fighting lasted four hours, the victims numbering 1000, mostly killed.'"

In a letter to her sister, also written at the end of November, KBF pointedly told her:

> Terror still reigns. The bazaars & schools are still closed & no one knows what the end will be. It appears that

> Turkey is in an uproar. Last week's "Daily News" spoke at length of the troubles in Bitlis, Erzeroum, Diabekir, Alleppo, Kharpont etc & there were a few leading articles, one of which prophecies terrible things for residents in Turkey if something is not done soon. For my part I wish one thing or the other would happen in Van. I am tired of waiting to be massacred. As far as we can see now the prospect is that we will all decamp in the spring. Would you like to see me home next summer? Dr. K. says she thinks there is no doubt that if we are alive we will go home. I am only beginning to work & I confess I should be sorry to have to leave our school & other work.

But even her predicament does not blind her to the much more desperate situations faced by Armenians.

> You should see the crowds of naked & starving villagers which fill our garden every morning. Dr. Kimball has opened a bakery in connection with her industrial department & she is now distributing clothing which the workers have been manufacturing. Friday I went down stairs to watch the distribution. Each one had to give his or her story & have it verified by the Rais [leader or chief] of the village before he could receive clothing & a ticket for bread. The stories were pitiful beyond words. People who a week before were well dressed & had everything a villager's heart could desire were utterly homeless & naked, starving. Many had lost their husbands & fathers, others their children & so forth.....
>
> During the summer & fall I did not speak of the conditions of affairs here but it is no use trying to put

> a bright face forward. As Dr. K. says the time for that is past & if we write from the very spot that the papers exaggerate, etc., how can we expect the Christian world ever to wake up? The papers do not exaggerate, my dear, they do not tell half the truth. The state of things here is so bad that it would tax your imagination to believe some of the things that happen around us every day.
>
> In Van vicinity 160 villages have been utterly destroyed, some of the inhabitants have been killed, others carried off & still others left in a naked & starving condition. By the way please cut out Mr. Howards letter & send to me by letterpost you may speak out as freely as you like in your letters. You notice that we have got beyond caring whether our words are read by the Turks or not.

KBF was heartened by the growing donations to the American Fund, which were a tremendous help to their relief efforts. In her journal, however, she wondered whether their efforts were truly humanitarian or simply a delay before a death more horrible than that by starvation or exposure.

> Last Friday 1 P.M. I spent an hour in the dispensary watching the crowds receive bread tickets & clothing. It was heartsickening to hear the stories told by the different people & the utter misery written on their faces was pitiful in the extreme. Almost every one had lost some one in the general fight & hurry to flee, some their husbands, others wives, others reported small boys missing.... One poor woman who had a few days before everything that a villagers heart could desire, who had been rich enough to feed 30 people from her table every

> day, came in with several little children utterly ragged & weeping the loss of their Father. Another woman tried to flee with her three children but found that she could not carry them all, so taking all the clothes which she could spare from her already almost naked body, she wrapped these around the oldest, a little boy about 5 years old & putting him among the rocks to wait her return from the city. Then she put a second one on her back & carrying the 3rd in her arms reached the city. Left her 2 littles ones & started back for the 3rd. When she reached the spot she found the dear little chap had died, perhaps from fright, as it was really not cold enough for the child to freeze.

We now know that hunger and scant clothing could result in the death by exposure in temperatures above freezing, especially for such a small child.

Close to the end of November, word reached KBF and her colleagues about the death of a former student, referred to only as "Jendy." Part of a small group of rebels (KBF didn't identify his affiliation with any particular faction), he crossed the border (presumably with Persia), heading for Van. The enterprise seemed doomed from the start when the group lost their way and were spotted by Kurds. Surrounded, Jendy's group "fought for their lives" before fleeing under cover of darkness. But the Kurds remained in hot pursuit, following them to a person whom she identified as Boghos, whom the American journalist William Willard Howard described in his own account as "the headman of the large and important village Boghos Kessan." Sheltered by villagers there, the group enjoyed a three-hour respite until a villager betrayed their location to the Kurds, who surrounded the dwelling.

The Kurds climbed to the roof and discharged their weapons through the smoke hole. Jendy and his comrades returned fire, forcing the Kurds off the roof. This success was short-lived, as the Kurds piled straw and other combustible items around the house and set it on fire. As the Armenians fled, the Kurds did not fire on them, though their guns were trained on the door. They preferred hand-to-hand combat. The Armenians cut down a few of the Kurds, but most were interested in taking the Kurds' horses in an attempt to flee. Jendy, however, was killed, after which "they mutilated his body." Out of the original group of fifty men, only twelve made it to Van. In revenge for the attack, the Kurds destroyed the village, "killing...and torturing a great many of the people, among them an old priest over 100 years old, whom they cut up and threw into the tonier." According to William Willard Howard, Boghos "was put to death in the prison at Van by the crushing of his private parts."

The brevity of KBF's journal entry for December 3, 1895, conveys anguish bordering on hopelessness: "City full of refugees & everyday our yard is packed. Yesterday Dr. K. told us how the priest at Khizan [*sic*] was killed. After life taken by most excruciating means, the skin was taken off the body & filled with straw." Then she added a line: "Naked woman on lakeshore gave birth to a child."

As the year 1895 drew to a close, KBF wrote to her sister: "Another year has almost been numbered with the past, and what a year it has been. The history of 1895 will not be very pleasant study for school children. Such a record seems altogether out of place in the 19th century. It ought to be placed away back in Tamerlane's time, for sure Ahmed Hamid 2nd has been almost equally cruel with that gory hero."

Continuing tensions and reports of violence and suffering that KBF found almost incomprehensible made for a bleak

Christmas of 1895. "This is Xmas morning but there is not Xmas cheer in the air. I can't realize that it is really Xmas day." KBF's spirits lifted somewhat upon receiving a cable from home at four o'clock that afternoon. "I cannot tell you how much that cablegram means to me. It makes you all seem so very near. And this last Xmas particularly it meant a great deal, indeed it was the only bit of Xmas cheer in the whole day."

The mission learned, ten days before Christmas, that the British vice consul, Cecil Hallward, was leaving for Diyarbekir after the massacre of five thousand people there. KBF wrote that after deriving such safety and security from his presence, they all "hate to lose him and hate especially to have him go to such a place. I hope the new man will be half so nice."

On Christmas Day, KBF wrote to her sister: "We are beginning to hope that Van will not have a turn at real bloodshed. There has been enough talk about it. The city is full of refugees. Dr. K. has already registered 4300. Some of them had wheat buried in their villages & have returned home but she is now giving rations to 2400 people daily. Aside from these the Industrial Bureau is supplying work to 900 families which represent 4500 souls."

Russian troops gathered at the Persian border, and although Turkish soldiers amassed to prevent them from entering the country, the vali confided to Hallward that there was not enough money in the treasury to arm them for very long. Regardless, everyone in the mission knew that wherever the first shot came from, a lack of funds would lead to bloodshed all around.

The mission's lack of cheer also derived from the decision to send the women and children to Persia as soon as possible, before the snow made roads utterly impassable. Where once KBF claimed the risk of flight was greater than the risk of remaining in Van, officials now determined flight to be the lesser risk. KBF and her colleagues "went to bed that night almost sick over the prospect. In the morning, we of the Spinsteran [*sic*] had a proposal ready for the station to the effect that Mrs. Reynolds [*sic*] and Mrs. Allen who cannot travel fast should go, and they could go on the pretext of a visit—and that we [KBF, Dr. Kimball, and their female colleagues] should remain as fast as the men if worse came to worse. You see, for us all to get out would sow terror in the hearts of our Armenian friends."

In a letter to Sadie, KBF wrote more of the women's rationale for remaining: "[W]e old maids can pack up at short notice and travel as fast as the men can." Their resistance and arguments paid off. The wives and children were to leave Van. KBF and her colleagues were to remain as long as the men stayed at their posts.

Chapter Eight

"I think I would be a Revolutionist myself"

Reassurances from the vali that he would do "all he can" to prevent an outbreak of violence were cold comfort for those left at the Van mission in January 1896. Even more discouraging was KBF's impression that "the Christians of Europe do not intend to do anything even if all their Asiatic brethren are swept from the earth."

With Cecil Hallward's removal to Diyarbekir approaching at the end of January, the man chosen to replace the British vice consul was a senior military officer. He was not a diplomat, but in KBF's opinion, he was "the man for the place... [selected] until the country is settled a bit." Major W. H. Williams arrived in January 1896 with his private secretary, Mr. Wilfred Thesiger, son of 2nd Baron Chelmsford and grandson of 1st Baron Chelmsford, twice Lord Chancellor of Britain. A young man of twenty-five who was just beginning a career in the military and then diplomatic circles, Thesiger was dubbed

"The Kid" by Dr. Kimball. KBF described him in a letter to Sadie as "tall & well built and has most charming manners." She was even more delighted to learn that he enjoyed horseback riding and was happy to take Cecil Hallward's place as her riding companion. Though their class and backgrounds might prevent any romance from flourishing (if either had any such inclination), Thesiger's company was a most welcome diversion for KBF.

Over the course of the autumn, KBF had been discouraged by Rev. Allen from making her daily forays into the countryside. Initially, he relented and permitted her to ride out in the company of one of the servants. But as autumn turned to winter, he deemed even that arrangement unsafe. Rev. Allen had agreed, though reluctantly, to her forays with Cecil Hallward. With the presence of new military men in the mission compound, KBF was both relieved and delighted to know that one of her last remaining simple pleasures was to continue, at least for the time being, in the company of Mr. Thesiger. Even that, however, wasn't without incident. During the course of one of their outings, "a lordly Kurd was splashed by a European rider...& is trying to make a fuss about it. The blame lies between Mr. T. & myself." KBF's tone has a touch of smug delight.

News arrived that Mr. Howard remained in Persia, sponsored by the *Christian Herald* and still hopeful of entering Turkey to deliver donations raised by the American Fund. Where once KBF expressed support for Mr. Howard, she now felt irritation. Although grateful for the money, KBF was annoyed that the *Christian Herald* sent Howard as their personal emissary to get a story for their paper. To make matters worse, he tried to convince Rev. Allen to meet him in Persia and accompany him to Van. Howard seemed more interested in getting a story than the risks that might be incurred by those he presumed to defend through his articles. Everyone was certain that Rev. Allen would refuse, knowing that to agree would bring unwanted scrutiny to the Van mission from Turkish officials who were equally intent that Howard not gain entry. KBF sympathized with Howard's frustration at not being permitted to enter the country, but she bristled at the thought that someone who had visited the country a few times relied mostly on the accounts of others (doubtless including her own) for his publications. KBF expressed disdain that the newspaper sent "a man from America to do the work that Dr. Kimball can do better than any Mr. Howard." KBF's words foreshadow similar words the British consul would use a few years later to describe her own work in Bulgaria, words that eventually became her epitaph.

As if the constant threat of violence weren't enough to try everyone's nerves, February 1896 brought earthquakes to Van and the surrounding area. The first arrived on February 3 as KBF and her colleagues sat down to their evening meal. "[W]hile we were sitting at dinner, we were startled by a slight jar of the table, then the dishes began to clatter, the walls to strain, and bits of plaster to fall." The tremors continued for about a minute—the longest duration of any quake since KBF had been in Van. It left them "limp and pale," but everyone soon recovered and continued with the meal. Later that evening, while KBF was engaged in activities with the female residents at the school, came aftershocks. KBF counted eleven of them up to midnight. One was sufficiently severe to cause several houses to collapse, one just a few hundred feet from the mission compound. Fortunately, no one was hurt.

The following day brought two more earthquakes, causing KBF to remark, "It gives one a very awful sensation when Mother Earth refuses to bear one calmly on her bosom." To make matters worse, Mother Nature brought two back-to-back snowstorms. Perhaps because snow was more familiar to KBF than earthquakes, she was at least able to appreciate the beauty of the plain and mountains in "their robe of dazzling white."

Earthquakes and aftershocks continued sporadically throughout February, so relief was immense when things quieted down in March. Attacks and skirmishes between soldiers and Revolutionists, however, continued—and with them grew increased risk to those who ventured into the streets. A Turkish soldier was killed; Armenians going about their business were attacked and stoned; houses were searched. An elder from a nearby village who visited the mission to ask for clothing for his people was stopped on his return journey by Turkish soldiers who beat him to death and took the clothing. One of the Armenian physicians set out from the mission for the city centre, but she was told by people returning from the city to turn back or risk attack. According to Major Williams, all sides were well-armed and apparently waiting for someone else to fire the first shot.

An Armenian family of five—a man and four children—sought refuge in the mission compound on March 7. Formerly well-to-do, the family's means were now "greatly reduced until now starvation seems the only outlook...all of them almost naked, thin clothing hanging in shreds about them.... [T]he poor ragged creatures huddled around the tonier warming their toes and at the same time eating as if they hadn't seen food for weeks." KBF was shocked to learn that two of the children, ages eleven and ten, whom she took to be brother and sister, were actually husband and wife and had been married for three years. The little girl dutifully waited on her eleven-year-old husband under the watchful eye of the patriarch.

Things seemed even more bleak when word reached the Van mission that Rev. George Knapp had been arrested and was to be taken from Bitlis to Constantinople to face charges and a trial. Everyone hoped that the sternest punishment meted out would be banishment from the country. In the same letter where KBF shared this news with her sister, she also noted that "Dr. Kimball is also in bad odour with his majesty" because of the continuing questions about the validity of her medical credential. In the next breath, KBF assured her sister that, regardless, the relief work would continue.

The rollercoaster of calm and violence continued throughout March. KBF feared, however, that because the bread supply was being cut, there would be "a large number of desperate men in Van" if relief ran out altogether. Word reached them that Nestorians (members of a branch of Eastern Christianity) in the mountains agreed to join forces with Revolutionists, and all were arming themselves with whatever came to hand, whether "short pieces of iron" or handguns.

In KBF's opinion, the greatest danger was not with the Turks but with the Kurds and the Revolutionists.

> The Revolutionists you know are divided into three parties: the "Hunchagists," the "Tashnagists" and "the Armenists." The Armenists are very moderate indeed and deserve the sympathy of good men, but the two former are red hot anarchists and the source of a good deal of danger. Yesterday we had very reliable word that they had united and were obtaining help from the Revolutionists among the Russian Armenians, with the view of making trouble on the border. We know that the numbers of the first two societies are working tooth and nail here in Van, and vow that if help does

not come in a few weeks from outside, they will throw another brand on the smouldering fire. It is said they are negotiating with the mountain Nestorians for help. They are almost like the Kurds and would strengthen the hands of the Hunchagists to a wonderful degree.

So much for their side. On the part of the Kurds, there is deep hatred for the Armenians, more especially against the Revolutionists, and they have sworn revenge for the loss of twenty men last fall. I think I told you about the Boghos Cassan affair, where in a fight between fifty Revolutionists and some Kurds, twenty of the latter were killed. Later the Kurds gathered, and after torturing some of the people most fiendishly, even cutting one poor old man up and throwing him into the tonier, they wiped the village out of existence. But their revenge was not complete and they swear to have it in the spring. Some of the chiefs were called in a couple of weeks ago before the Van officials and were ordered in public to be good boys and play gently. Afterwards, they were entertained by the same officials and told to go ahead and do as they liked. At least this is the story some of the Kurds have told their Armenian friends in the city and to give it an appearance of truth, the same men amused themselves on their way home cracking the skull of one poor creature, robbing a party of seven, breaking an arm of another villager, and sticking a knife into their last victim.

A third element of danger is from the refugees and starving Vanlees. Until now they have had help, but the stream from which the gold comes was not a Pastolus and now the bread rations are being cut down. Many

> names are being erased entirely from the books. Dr. Kimball said it was the hardest thing she ever did when Saturday, many who had been receiving help were turned away. They thanked her with trembling lips for past help but immediately a desperate look crossed their faces and some said "a piece of cold iron will be our last resource." They are giving way to a feeling of desperation.
>
> Our Vali is a good man we all think, but the soldiers do not like him and it is said the warm feeling formerly shown between him and the Ferrik Pasha (commander of the troops) is giving place to strained relations.

Clara Barton of the American Red Cross arrived in Constantinople in February 1896 to distribute aid and do her best to bolster the spirits of those doing missionary work in Turkey. She hoped to deliver her message in person, but based on her own knowledge of the situation in Turkey, KBF was not convinced Barton would travel as she wished. "She has not yet received her papers and the Turks are adept at procrastination. It is not likely that she will ever get her travelling papers. She is distributing through the missionaries at present. And Sir Philip Currie says that is what ought to have been done in the first place. It was foolish to expect permission from the Sultan to travel freely in Turkey, especially after Mr. Howard's failure."

Though grateful for the efforts of people like Barton and Howard, KBF's correspondence during this time conveys frustration that borders on resentment. But as a well-mannered and educated woman, she did not permit herself the outright expression that, though newspapers and charitable organizations send people to Turkey for a few days or weeks, those who had lived in the country and worked alongside its Armenian citizens were in a better position to talk about what was happening in the country. To speak of one's own involvement, particularly if one was a woman, seemed like ego inflation, and KBF was careful to avoid it. She was far more likely to give credit to Grace Kimball—and she did, repeatedly.

Melting snows in April brought anticipated escalation of attacks by the Kurds against Armenian communities. On April 1, KBF wrote of an attack on three villages in which twenty-five men were killed. The mutasarrif expressed outrage and promised Major Williams the perpetrators would be brought to justice. "The Armenians do not believe in his promises as freely as Major W. does, but let us hope they are in the wrong. Anyway, everything depends on what is done in the next few days. If the big Kurds are arrested and punished severely, all will be well. If not, then there will be trouble of a very serious nature."

That last sentence seems to mark a shift in KBF's thinking about the Armenians' situation. And if it does not and was instead a heartfelt expression of what she had thought for a long time, then she was emboldened to express it openly, regardless—as she wrote in a letter the previous month—of possible reprisals by Turkish officials who opened and read their mail.

KBF remained keen to teach the children about Protestant Christianity and Western ways. She held a dinner party for some of the young men who were students at the school and was suitably impressed with their ability to eat with forks and knives, even though "others, perhaps, use their fingers more than forks for conveying food to the mouth." They were joined at table by Grace Knapp and Wilfred Thesiger, and KBF felt amused at the notion that the latter "was shocked more or less during the evening for I am sure he had never been to such a dinner party before, I mean, where the guests were of such mixed character."

The evening was a success, and after enjoying ice cream, the party broke up at ten thirty, concluding with the singing of several revolutionary songs. Thesiger was not conversant in the Armenian language, and KBF felt that "had he understood the words he would have been shocked beyond words, they were so full of the spirit of revenge." Concerned for the young men's safety (all were approximately nineteen or twenty years of age, so a likely target of violence), KBF and Thesiger walked them to the schoolroom to spend the night in the safety of the compound. Before bed that night, KBF wrote, "I think I would be a revolutionary myself—of the Armenist type—if I were an Armenian."

Part of KBF's teaching duties included music instruction for students in both the boys' and girls' schools and extended to some of the teaching staff who had "fair voices." Inspired by the resident talent, KBF felt moved to go beyond the usual Protestant hymns and include some of the Armenian liturgical music with which she had become familiar and liked very much. In addition to the Easter hymns sung in four-part harmony, the group prepared two sharakans or chants. "The Armenians are very fond of their Old Church music but for some reason it has never been introduced into our Protestant church but we hope after this that a Sharakan will always be sung at morning service."

Rev. Allen grew increasingly more alarmed with new reports of violence and took "it into his head that he is going whether we have to leave Van or not, and with that view in mind has packed almost all his belongings...but the Vali thought travelling was very inadvisable at present and so he remains at home. We laugh at him for having things packed up and living so uncomfortably."

Rather than packing up their belongings, KBF and her colleagues decide to teach themselves how to play tennis. Even Dr. Kimball, who worked long hours and drove herself to the brink of exhaustion, agreed to learn. "[W]e are anticipating lots of fun always providing the Kurds do not come."

April brought more loss, and of a more personal nature. In the early stages of her second pregnancy, Satinug—the young teacher whose wedding KBF and Dr. Kimball had attended just three years earlier—had contracted typhoid. Terribly weakened, a decision was made to abort the child in the hopes of saving the young woman's life. Initially, "she grew ever so much better and we all rejoiced that our dear Satinug—for we all loved her—was on the highroad to recovery. But alas! She took cold, rheumatic fever set in and struck to her heart, taking her off rather suddenly this morning." Satinug's distraught husband desired nothing more than to take their only surviving child, an eighteen-month-old son, to the United States. KBF wrote in her journal: "Many people are trying to get out of the country. If the road was open & the people were free to go home, blessed it would be." As it was, "There has been another suicide this week & probably there will be many more. People are so hopeless."

Increasing threats of armed uprisings overshadowed private grief. KBF reported the murder of a man on the path over which she rode her horse each day. Another was stabbed in the back on his way to the city. And "[t]oday, the body of a poor, half-foolish man was brought in all hacked in a most brutal manner." She was heartsick to learn that the horrific murder came at the hands of a soldier and a zaptieh. She saw people "armed to the teeth"—one man with cartridge belts, ammunition, "a short sword and revolver, besides his rifle. The rest of the costume was very picturesque and the man himself was very handsome. He had been through a good many trying scenes.... I should imagine he will fight like a demon."

Although KBF had declared that she did not care who read her letters, she had sober second thoughts upon learning that William Dennis, editor of the *Halifax Herald*, contacted her sister, asking to publish them. Though she thought his request was "very impudent," she asked when her sister planned to send excerpts in exchange for a ten dollar donation to Armenian relief. She wondered, "Who under the sun wanted to see my picture anyway. I didn't come out to Van to gain such notoriety. Anyway, what have I done to deserve it?" In the end, she neither agreed nor declined. Despite this, excerpts from her letters appeared in Halifax, Yarmouth, and even Boston. It's possible KBF felt it necessary to protest the publication of her letters because she knew Turkish government officials read many of them. This possibility gains more credence upon examining her Psalmist in the Nova Scotia Archives, in which KBF pasted copies of the published articles and the notes she wrote to pen them.

Rev. Allen's desire to quit Van increased on April 19 after he received a telegram from Urmia, Persia, informing him that his wife had given birth to a son. But he remained in Turkey and agreed to accompany George Knapp's remaining family from Bitlis to reunite them in Constantinople. KBF was surprised, bordering on shocked, that Grace Knapp hesitated to accompany Rev. Allen to be reunited with her family. "She has a quixotic idea that she will soon be able to go back to Bitlis even if her family is not there. We do not think that there is one chance in a hundred for her return.... She will have to decide today but none of us feel like influencing her decision for fear she will think we do not appreciate her presence here.... Doctor has spoken to her."

For everyone at the Van mission, the daily uncertainty of what would happen and the expectation that, no matter what happened, the outcome would not be good, was exhausting. Toward the end of April KBF wrote:

> We are still on the eve of trouble. I wish it would get night or morning or something to change this awful suspense. The revolutionists are making extensive preparations for an attack on the Kurds in the region extending from Shadag to the Persian border and they propose to do to them just what the Kurds did to the Armenians last fall. It will be a perfectly suicidal course for them to take but they are certainly going in for it.... They really are very strong now and are very well armed.... There is scarcely an Armenian in Van now who is not in sympathy with the movement. It was not so a few months ago but the utter hopelessness of their condition has driven them to it....
>
> Our circle is gradually getting small again. Next week we shall be only four. Mr. Allen last week tried to make us believe that we would go out with the Russians when they go about the middle of May. I think now we shan't go but there is no telling what may happen any day. One hour we talk plans for future work, the next we feel that we shall have to leave. You cannot have any idea of the terrible state things are in here. It isn't easy to do one's work as it should be done when one feels that at any moment it may all be stopped.
>
> The snow is going slowly from the mountains this spring, doubtless postponing the evil day which

> everyone says is sure to come.... The relief work is being carried on as vigorously as ever. Poor Dr. Kimball is getting so tired. She said at dinner this evening that 22,000 are now receiving help. Yesterday, two or three hundred came in from Shadag, about the worst looking creatures that have come to us yet. Shadag used to be one of the most prosperous regions. Now it is in as bad, if not worse condition than the others.

An attack on the mission's dispensary in early May only added to the jittery nerves of KBF and her colleagues, given that the dispensary was on the ground floor and sleeping quarters were upstairs. The perpetrator smashed a window by throwing a rock through it, then soaked a rag in oil, lit it, and threw it through the window. A night watchman sent up the alarm and the building was evacuated without incident. Major Williams "represented the matter very strongly to the Vali," and another guardhouse was quickly built on the property and an additional night watchman installed, leaving KBF feeling "as safe as possible now."

Grace Knapp finally decided to reunite with her family. Accordingly, she accompanied Rev. Allen to Constantinople. On May 4, 1896, KBF recorded in her journal: "Mr. Allen & Miss Knapp left Friday A.M....for Erzeroum. Station now reduced to four." After Allen's and Knapp's departure, word reached KBF and her colleagues that at a stopover in Diyarbekir in early April, Grace's father, George Knapp, had not been permitted to stay with Mr. Hallward and instead was held "under a vigilant watch" in a guardhouse in the city, presumably to ensure that Knapp behaved himself.

In a letter written by Mr. Hallward to British Biblical scholar and philanthropist Professor James Rendel Harris, the former doesn't disguise his suspicion of Turkish authorities' detention of George Knapp, going so far as to invoke Shakepeare's *Julius Caesar*: "I should like to see Knapp's indictment, the Turks excel in that branch of literature, they breathe such an air of sweet simplicity of transparent candour into such documents that the unwary stranger thinks they must be 'all—all honourable men,' quite incapable of stooping to any baseness."

Once the Knapp family was finally reunited, they continued on to the United States. Grace Knapp eventually returned to Turkey where she remained for several years and provided a first-hand account of the genocide in 1915.

In the meantime, someone whom KBF referred to as "Shakir the Outlaw" wreaked havoc in the area around Van. Although the mutasarrif ventured forth with the promise to bring the Kurds to justice, he returned with "seven or eight hundred liras" in fines and none of the "sixty men in chains" he had promised to bring. "Shakir is still acting his pleasure... [and] making life a hell upon earth for the poor villagers." The men whom Dr. Kimball was sending out with help to Shadag went one day's journey and then came back because they had heard such rumours about Shakir's doings. "Such ups and downs. One day we feel everything will surely be settled peacefully. The next, the air fairly quivers with alarm."

On May 27, KBF hastily recorded three brief lines in her journal: "Hospital cases: one with 30 wounds finally died of lockjaw. Woman shot and baby born afterwards. Many neck and hand wounds, bad fractures, etc."

Finally, in early June, tensions came to a head and fighting broke out in a quarter of Van that KBF referred to as "Arak." Fighting quickly spread, and reports of "massacring, robbing, and burning" reached the mission. Major Williams ventured out to determine the threat level. In a letter written by Cecil Hallward to Professor James Rendel Harris on July 26, 1896, Hallward reported that KBF wrote to him and "spoke of most disastrous chances...of 'moving accidents,' or 'hairbreadth escapes,' among the latter being Major Williams from a bullet fired at him in the street. She doesn't explain how the row began, but the fighting lasts from June 15 to 23—fighting in the streets, massacring, burning, etc.—no. of killed unknown, many houses within town burnt and enormous plunder by soldiers and zaptiés [*sic*].... If the Consul had been killed, she says scarcely a Christian woman would have been left alive in the town."

Reporting on the first night of what would become a nine-day battle, KBF wrote in her journal, "things quieted a bit & there were only sporadic shots during the night." The following morning, although there was no more shooting, palls of smoke indicated that many houses had been set ablaze and that "the trouble was not yet over." Around ten o'clock, Turks and Revolutionists engaged in a gun battle that went on for several hours. "Towards evening we were told that the Kurds were coming the next morning and we went to bed with that pleasing prospect to dream over."

Gunfire throughout the night prevented a good night's sleep, and by five A.M. on June 17 KBF "was glad enough to get up." An hour later, Major Williams appeared "with a 'Union Jack.' The dear old flag. I hugged it. Major laughed and told me to go wrap it around the others who were still in bed, to make them feel that they were going to be protected, but instead I went and flung it to the breeze from the corner of our roof, in lieu of a better place until a flagstaff could be expected." In a letter written several months later, Cecil Hallward noted that taking the Union Jack into the mission compound and KBF waving it atop the building provided a clear message to all that the compound was British territory and that any attack upon it would constitute a severe diplomatic breach. Evidently, the local people understood the statement, too. KBF explained what happened next:

> A little later, an order was given by the Major for all... to find refuge on the mission premises and the crowd began to surge in. Many came flying as if for life without any impediments. Some came bowed down with piles of bedding, while still others not willing to lose anything came staggering under the weight of great copper dishes and heavy boxes. The excitement was terrific, everyone struggling for the best place and all seeming to think that safety was only to be found in our houses.
>
> Just before 11 A.M., about 200 hundred mounted Kurds were seen coming from the south towards the city. The Major went out to see the Mutesarif [*sic*] about sending out soldiers to turn them back. There was a good deal of shooting and burning during the day, but toward evening it again quieted, and as the Kurds had been driven out, safety was proclaimed for the nearest Armenians to go to their homes for the night. Many went, but a very large crowd remained. After midnight, firing between the Turks and Revolutionists was almost incessant and in the morning all the people who had gone home to spend the night came back.

Several years later, in December 1900, Beatrice Chamberlain, sister of the future prime minister of Britain, Neville Chamberlain, met Grace Kimball while touring the United States. Chamberlain wrote to her sister that during the June 1896 attack, Kimball stood "all day in the doorway with a pistol in her hand to protect the women & children in the house behind her [because] The soldiers did not dare to attack an American." According to Kimball, "Major Williams...snatched a fez from a soldier and gave orders in Turkish, which caused them to think he was one of their officers, so they obeyed him." Thus he saved many lives.

In the evening of the first day of the nine-day attack, Major Williams sent a telegram to the English embassy in Constantinople, asking the British, French, and Russian embassies to "try to persuade the Sultan to pardon all the rebels if ten of their number would deliver themselves and all their arms to the Major." In exchange, Major Williams promised to conduct them all out of the country. After sending the telegram, he contacted the Revolutionists to ask if they would agree to abide by the terms. They promised an answer in the morning. Everyone went to bed that evening anxious but hopeful that the proposal would be accepted.

But the expected answer did not come in the morning. Instead, more gunfire was exchanged and Major Williams narrowly escaped a bullet (likely the incident that Cecil Hallward wrote about in his July letter to Professor Harris). Word arrived that the number of Revolutionists to be conducted out of the country by Major Williams was increased to sixty. The Revolutionists grudgingly agreed and, according to KBF, "an armistice was concluded until the Sultan's answer should come. But the most imminent danger is now from Kurds, 10,000 of whom had surrounded the city."

> The officials feared they might not be able to keep them back but they promised to do everything possible. The Major acknowledged that the outlook was very black but he hoped to pull us thro'. No one went home that night and orders were given to bring as much wheat as possible

into the place the next morning. Thro' the night there was almost incessant shooting. The soldiers had broken the armistice.

When I came out of my room Saturday morning, Hadji called me to come and see the Kurds on Taprakalli. In a few minutes they had descended upon Ungooznen quarter, sharp shooting followed and a little later five fires were going in that one little corner. The shooting came nearer to us, balls whizzed past our house, and the guard ordered the north windows cleared of people.

Then we discovered that cannon were being used. Shells fell quite near. One passed through the roof of the consulate and fell into the dining room without bursting. One tore up the earth at the foot of our hill and made a bit of a dust. More and more fires started up until the air was thick with smoke, while shooting never ceased. This to the north of us.

Over towards Arak the shooting was heavier than at any previous time.... At about 11 A.M. we discovered 4 Katchaks [a Turkish word for contraband, though in this context KBF uses it to describe illegal or banned persons] trying to steal their way around the vineyard at the foot of our hill, to join their friends in the grove where the heavy shooting was taking place. Our guard and Dr. K. rushed out to tell them not to fire. Mr. Thesiger also ordered them to desist but in a second every gun was discharged [which] caused a panic among the people on the grounds.

All the morning, Armenians from every quite distant quarter had been pouring in occupying every available

> inch of space. Our house was so full that we almost feared the floors would fall in. After lunch I counted 1100 under our roof. Doctor said there were more than 15,000 on the premises.

Major Williams, accompanied by Turkish soldiers, visited the vali to inquire whether any word had come from the Sultan concerning his proposal. When he hadn't returned by nightfall, KBF and her colleagues were almost frantic with worry. At last he appeared, bringing news that "the Sultan would not accept ten or even 60 Katchaks." Instead, all would have to lay down their arms and report to the citadel. Major Williams brought together the leaders of the uprising, none of whom would agree to the terms. Around midnight, about one thousand "Katchaks" fled Van, less than half bearing arms—many of them merely boys, some of them KBF's students. In hot pursuit were Kurds and Turkish soldiers.

If those in the mission thought the departure of the Katchaks would achieve peace, they were sorely disappointed. At breakfast the next morning, word arrived that both Turkish soldiers and Kurds were plundering whatever was left and setting houses on fire. Dense smoke obscured views in every direction as heavy gunfire continued. Around noon, when a ball landed inside the compound, a panicked cry went up that their own soldiers were firing upon them. To add to the mayhem, word got around that the Kurds were at the gates. Women screamed and fainted, and KBF feared a stampede would ensue. With great effort, a measure of calm was restored, but the flow of people seeking shelter increased throughout the day. KBF estimated their numbers at twenty thousand.

Although several ovens had been installed in a couple of locations in the mission compound to bake bread for the relief effort, only one was deemed to be in a location sufficiently safe and secure to use. With only one oven in operation, it was impossible to feed the crowd of people who were close to starvation even before fleeing to the compound. "Towards evening, the misery was increased by a heavy shower of rain," KBF wrote in a letter to her sister Tina. "The doors had to be locked to keep out the crowds, for we greatly feared that our floors would fall in if the number increased. Some of the people had regular tents, others fixed up blankets, gorgeous quilts, shawls and beautiful rugs using as a framework some lumber which we fortunately had on hand. The scene from our roof was an exceedingly picturesque one but one could not forget the awful misery of the wretched crowd long enough to give play to one's sense of the artistic."

While people in the mission prayed for the violence to end, Major Williams and Mr. Thesiger tried desperately—and for the most part, fruitlessly—to make everyone lay down their arms. Instead, Williams and Thesiger fled for their lives after coming across a "rabble" that had hacked to death two hundred Armenians. They found cover until they deemed it sufficiently safe to return to the mission, all the while wondering about the safety of the mission's inhabitants.

The vali restored calm but the next day conducted searches of the homes that remained standing, looking for Katchaks and weapons. He also insisted that every man and boy be turned out of the mission. "[The women] thought that their fathers and brothers were going out to death and the consequent crying and screaming were most trying. One woman came to me and begged me for some poison."

At ten thirty, "the excitement rose to a terrific pitch" with the sudden appearance of Hamdieh Kurds "almost next door to the consulate. Major was already there. Mr. Thesiger buckled on his cartridges, snatched his rifle and ran. A few minutes later there was a good deal of sharp shooting, and we all sat in breathless expectancy. Would the Kurds pass up the hill or not? Those were the most trying minutes. Every shot made me fear that one or both of our English protectors would be killed which would mean death to all on our premises."

Their efforts to repel the Kurds were supported by the man KBF calls Ferrik Pasha, a local Turkish military officer, and after more gunfire, the Kurds were on the run, with Turkish soldiers in pursuit. Around four o'clock, they watched with great relief and some pleasure "the Kurds leaving the city by the hundreds." An hour later, it was declared safe for people to return to their homes, "but most feared to leave their safe retreat and we did not urge anyone to go against his will."

The departing Kurds weren't about to go quietly, burning villages on their flight path. Turkish soldiers in pursuit of the Kurds did not behave any better, and some felt they used their pursuit of the Kurds as cover to plunder any village they came across. On reaching Varagavank they brutally killed the abbot and threw his remains to the dogs. One woman watched in horror as her two young sons were butchered with an axe. Estimates of the number of Armenians killed in Van alone was between five and six hundred, with a far greater toll when the fatalities in the surrounding communities were added to it.

Finally, word came from the Sultan that he would guarantee safe passage for the rebels to Persia in exchange for cessation of hostilities. At first, the Armenian combatants were understandably reluctant. Major Williams helped to assure them he trusted the Sultan's word, coming as it had at the urging of the English, French, and Russian embassies. Nearly one thousand young Armenian men laid down their arms and accepted an escort of Turkish soldiers to march to Persia. Not far from Van, they were set upon by Turkish soldiers and by Kurds, who massacred the unarmed men.

News of the slaughter shocked everyone, especially Major Williams who had taken the Sultan at his word and given his assurances to the young Armenian men. Violence in the outlying villages continued. When Major Williams filed his report late in June, he estimated that some 20,000 Armenians had been killed and some 350 communities destroyed.

As fear and attacks escalated, loyalties became more difficult to determine. Dr. Raynolds wrote to his wife, Martha, who later shared the news in the Woman's Board of Missions' newsletter, *Life and Light for Women*, that one of the schoolgirls who had been permitted to leave the mission to visit family was stopped in the streets on her way back and discovered to be carrying cartridges. If this revelation shocked those at the mission school, they were appalled to learn a short time later that a member of the congregation permitted to visit her husband in Persia was found on the return journey carrying correspondence from Revolutionists. The fact that she carried her church membership—signed by Dr. Raynolds—called into question whether anyone else in the mission shared her sympathies. Members of the mission staff had taken great pains to remain as neutral as possible politically, while offering help to those in need. Now they weren't sure how local Turkish officials viewed them.

On July 1, 1896, KBF wrote her sisters that although things were quieter in Van, massacres continued in Armenian communities across eastern Turkey and the Kurds had not retreated far. "Our future is uncertain," she said. Even so, she signed off by telling her sisters, "don't worry about me."

The mission staff carried on, doing what they could—tending patients, teaching school—for the rest of the month, as the political situation continued to deteriorate. Halfway through July, Dr. Raynolds and Major Williams decided that it was time for most of the staff to leave Van. Major Williams's return to England was imminent, and they determined that Mr. Thesiger could not take sole responsibility for the care and safety of the remaining staff. Although Dr. Raynolds decided to remain through another winter, everyone else would depart on August 4. The route via Persia was no longer deemed safe, so their destination was Constantinople.

KBF hoped that their absence would be short-lived, perhaps only a matter of weeks or months in Constantinople. And if the decision was to send them all home, then "I have had three years & a half of very happy work here & it may be that the spring of '97 will see us back again. It doesn't seem possible that the station will be abandoned."

A widowed Armenian woman and her children, Makarid (on her back) and Nuvart (standing next to her). In 1899, after the murder of her husband in the aftermath of the Armenian Massacres of 1894–1896, the family walked from their home in the Geghi region to Kharpert (Harput), eastern Anatolia (Turkey) seeking help from missionaries. (LIBRARY OF CONGRESS, BAIN NEWS SERVICE PHOTOGRAPH COLLECTION, LC-DIG-GGBAIN-27081)

Chapter Nine

"I am ready to go anywhere else I can do good"

KBF and her colleagues left Van at 6:15 a.m. on August 4, 1896, accompanied by the Russian consul, Mr. Myefski, Wilfred Thesiger, and about forty Armenians who felt safer leaving with them than remaining in Van. KBF rode out on her horse, Ildemir. The group travelled until 7:00 p.m., setting up camp at a community KBF calls Janing, where they "[p]assed a comfortable night in our tents." Their journey the following day was shorter because, when they stopped to refresh themselves at Nain, the local Kurdish leader entreated them to be his guests for the night. Two of his wives were

> gotten up most gorgeously in rose and purple and gold brocade [with] caps...covered with gold coins and strings of gold hung from ear to ear around.... A yellow silk [scarf] was draped about the back of the head. Of course bracelets and the youngest wore a nose

> ring. Face uncovered in the house.... After passing the usual compliments and telling a good many fibs in the process, the women begged to be excused as they were going to see about our dinner. It had been decided that we would eat in the harem instead of with our own boys in the tent. By and by we were called out to a most excellent dinner and we did justice to it in Kurd fashion, fingers serving for forks, a few spoons were provided for the soups. After dinner...men allowed to go back to the kiosk but to my rejoicing, I found [the harem] would keep us with them all night. We had good beds at a pleasant sleeping place.

This is a far cry from KBF's initial assessments only four years earlier that so many of the country's customs—regardless of religious affiliation—were "barbaric." KBF also noted that this particular leader of the Kurds "is spoken of rather highly by the Armenians. He protected many during the last [raids]."

The group continued its journey, finding another generous Kurdish host the following night. In contrast, however, on the third night they were refused admittance to a Kurdish encampment. The night was marred by wet weather and no fodder for their horses. On approaching the Kurds who had refused them shelter to ask for food for the horses, they were told they could have some—for a price. Without enough tents for everyone, some of the party slept under the open sky. The winds whipped the heavy rains, soaking everyone regardless of whether they slept on the ground or on cots, in the open or under canvas. "We were glad to get up and off the next morning for we were cold and shivering. Presently the sun broke through the clouds and we all began to smile and feel cheerful again."

The remainder of their journey was tiring. They enjoyed an "elegant dinner...notwithstanding our riding habits" at the home of one official, and at one point while their baggage was detained for examination by customs officials, KBF had to make herself "comfortable without my nightdress and other toilet articles. However, we were all so sleepy and tired that we slept in spite of everything." In order to continue, however, it was necessary for them to sell some of their items, including KBF's beloved horse. The party continued in carriages, arriving in Constantinople on August 23, three days before the infamous bank incident.

Not even the barest wisp of cloud dotted the sky over Constantinople on August 26, 1896. High temperatures paralleled the tensions in the city as the three leaders of the Armenian Reform Party took to the streets with twenty-five armed activists of the Dashnaktsutyun Party. Not surprisingly, accounts of the day differ depending on the source consulted. Severe press censorship imposed by the Sultan in Constantinople did not prevent accounts from reaching other parts of the world, but even those were downplayed by the international press.

In one paper, the *South Australian Register*, there appeared two reports, dated August 27 and 28, and an editorial piece, all published in the August 29 edition. The reports described the occupation of the Ottoman Bank by the small group of protesters as having caused great damage, "wrecking many of the buildings" with "hundreds of civilians and several soldiers...killed." One report added, "Private accounts which have reached Berlin state that the Turks in retaliation for the riots butchered hundreds of Armenians." In fact, no Turkish soldiers were killed, while two of the Dashnaks perished in the attack.

The occupation of the Ottoman Bank was an attempt by Armenian activists to draw attention to the plight of Armenians living under Ottoman rule and encourage the Great Powers to help gain a measure of the freedom recently granted to Christians living under Ottoman rule in Crete.

Although the small group of activists (initial reports estimated their number at one hundred, when in fact there were only about twenty-five) managed to hold the bank against Turkish soldiers, they realized as the siege wore on that their means of escape grew increasingly limited. The gunpowder they carried would only make a small hole in the bank's wall, not enough to create a diversion that would allow them to escape. Despite the exchange of gunfire and bombs, they assured those trapped in the bank with them that their intention was not to rob the bank or harm any of the occupants but to bring international attention to their cause. Only the intervention of the Russian and French embassies persuaded the Sultan not to bomb the building—and all its occupants, regardless of faith or nationality—to rubble. Threatened with the retaliation of having his palace razed by guns on ships belonging to the Great Powers that were moored in the harbour, the Sultan relented. He agreed to permit the surviving activists to be escorted to the yacht belonging to the Ottoman Bank's English director, Sir Edgar Vincent, for safe passage to Marseille and thence to exile.

The departure of the activists did not end the bloodshed. Over the following two days, a heavy price was exacted from Armenians living in Constantinople. Soldiers and students dragged Armenians from their homes and businesses to be beaten or slaughtered in the streets. No one attempted to stop the revenge, until leaders from French, Russian, and British ships anchored in the harbour came ashore to demand a stop. With tensions remaining high, the group from Van decided to quit Constantinople altogether as soon as some order was restored. Even so, KBF held out hope that the situation would calm down enough to permit her to return to Constantinople, then to Van, in October.

KBF sailed for England on August 28 in the company of Grace Kimball and Elizabeth Huntingdon. Once in London, Grace Kimball boarded a ship back to the United States where, despite extensive tours of Europe and the Far East in the first decades of the twentieth century, she remained for the rest of her life. After her years in Armenia, she was apparently content to open a medical practice in the quiet community of Poughkeepsie, New York. There, she shared a house with her friend and partner (as listed in the 1920 census), Dr. Elizabeth Thelberg, a physician and an instructor at Vassar College who had raised funds for Kimball's work in Van.

Not long after Kimball embarked for home, Elizabeth Huntingdon left London for work with the International Institute in San Sebastian, Spain. Not yet ready to return home to Nova Scotia, KBF looked for a way to make herself useful in the growing efforts to assist Armenian refugees fleeing Turkey who were flooding into the port of Marseille. But what was to be done with them all?

Enter two women: Lady Henry Somerset (a Brit) and Frances Willard (an American). Though not solely responsible for the welfare of the hundreds of Armenian refugees flooding into the port of Marseille, they were certainly significant in contributing to their well-being and helping to coordinate relief efforts.

Approximately twenty years earlier, Lady Henry (born Isabella Caroline Somers-Cocks in 1851) caused a sensation when, upon discovering her husband was homosexual, she sued for divorce and for custody of their two-year-old son. Though homosexuality was a criminal offence in England, her actions defied social conventions of the time whereby what happened in middle- and upper-class homes was a private matter. A man's home was his castle, within which he assumed control over his wife's body, property, finances, actions, and movements, while she was expected to ignore any of her husband's "transgressions" in the interests of being a good wife and mother—whatever the cost.

Lady Henry Somerset made significant contributions to the relief efforts to assist Armenian refugees fleeing Turkey.
(LIBRARY OF CONGRESS, LC-USZ62-122280)

But it wasn't just divorce that brought scandal (Lord Henry moved to Italy, where he remained for the rest of his life) and made her a social outcast, it was her opinions about the cause and most effective treatments of alcoholism and drug dependency and her compassion for the poor and destitute, particularly women. She embraced the women's temperance movement and women's suffrage (though she condemned the use of violence). Instead of retiring from public life after her divorce, she established her residence near her birthplace, Eastnor Castle, in Ledbury, Herefordshire, where she set up a treatment centre for destitute women struggling with drug and alcohol dependency. She campaigned tirelessly throughout the country as the head of the British Women's Temperance Association, using her social contacts to raise awareness and funds. In 1913, she was voted by readers of the *Evening News* (London) as the woman they would most like to have as prime minister—had women been permitted to sit in the House of Commons. Her public addresses often drew thousands of people, and her reputation took her to the United States, where she met Frances Willard.

Though the women were more than ten years apart in age, they were soulmates when it came to their ardour for the women's temperance movement and social justice. At the age of thirty-two, Frances Willard (1839–1898) became president of the Evanston College for Ladies in 1871, just one year before a twenty-year-old Isabella Caroline Somers-Cocks walked down the aisle as the fresh-faced and naive bride of Lord Henry Somerset. When Evanston College merged with Northwestern University in 1873, Willard became Dean of Women at the Women's College. In 1874 (the year in which Lady Henry gave birth to her first and only child, named after his father), Willard resigned her position after a disagreement over governance with the university's president (and her former fiancé), Charles Henry Fowler. From this point, Willard began a

Frances Willard was a leading light in the causes of suffrage, temperance, and education and labour reforms.
(LIBRARY OF CONGRESS, LC-USZ61-790)

firm trajectory to becoming a leading light in the causes of suffrage, temperance, and education and labour reforms, starting with her involvement in the creation of the Chicago Women's Christian Temperance Union. She became its president in 1879. By the time she met Lady Henry, Willard was also president of the World's Woman's Christian Temperance Union and the National Council of Women of the United States.

A mutual friend saw the close parallels in both women's passionate commitment to women's suffrage and, knowing each was aware of the other's work, arranged for the two to meet in the US in 1891. It was a meeting of both mind and spirit, and a deep, loving relationship blossomed. For the next five years, they were almost inseparable, travelling together in the US and throughout Britain, using Lady Henry's estate at Reigate Priory as a home base and funding their travels with Lady Henry's deep (but limited, as time would tell) pockets. The pet names they gave one another weave through their correspondence: Lady Henry's for Willard were "Frank" or "Conk," and Willard's for Lady Henry were "Earl Cosmos" or "Cozzie." Each supported the work of the other and defended her staunchly against detractors. And at times when one didn't agree with the other, she offered thoughtful criticism, encouraging the other to change her mind. And when that was not possible, neither ever withdrew support for the other, instead remaining steadfast and constant.

By the time KBF met her in 1896, Lady Henry supported the temperance movement, international women's suffrage, birth control, and the licensing of prostitution in India in an effort to quell the spread of sexually transmitted diseases among British soldiers stationed in that country—none of which helped to heal the rift with "polite society," which stood in judgment of her. Frances Willard embodied the same values, condemning the lynchings that plagued the southern US despite advice that in doing so she risked alienating white southerners who might support and donate to her temperance cause. Never an apologist, she said the cause didn't want their money.

Though Lady Henry's health was far from robust, Willard's was of more immediate and persistent concern. She was diagnosed with pernicious anaemia, a condition that had killed her mother in 1892. Lady Henry spared no expense in providing support—from building a gym for Willard on her estate, to hiring a Dutch woman to be Willard's personal trainer. Lady Henry bought her a bicycle (which Willard nicknamed Gladys) to ensure she took daily exercise in fresh air along the paths Lady Henry laid out on the grounds of the Priory. At one point, when Willard's extended stay in England was criticized and her right to a salary from the US associations (the Chicago Woman's Christian Temperance Union and the National Council of Women of the United States) questioned, Lady Henry promptly made a donation in the amount of Willard's salary of the previous two years.

The bond between the two women was such that a month or so after Frances returned to the US in November 1896, leaving Lady Henry to her family and work in London, Frances wrote in her journal on December 31: "Why is there never word, sign or token? Why must Isabel and I be separated? Because we put our Work before our Love."

That separation became permanent with Willard's premature death in 1898. At the age of fifty-eight she contracted influenza shortly before she was to board a ship to take her back to England. Her funeral cortège started in New York and progressed to her final resting place in Chicago, with thousands turning out along the way to pay their respects. In the National Statuary Hall in Washington there is a statue commemorating

Frances Willard. A minority among statuary predominantly dedicated to men, she was selected by her home state, Illinois, as its best representation of itself. In contrast, when Lady Henry died in 1921, after a requiem mass that included floral tributes from Queen Mary and Queen Alexandra, she was buried quietly—at her request—in the churchyard of St. Alban's at Holborn instead of in her family's mausoleum. Eventually a memorial was erected, but it was stolen. In 1991, a statue—a young girl holding out a water bowl—dedicated to her was unveiled in London's Temple Gardens.

Working closely side by side, Willard and Lady Henry were a powerhouse pair, seemingly indefatigable despite health challenges, even writing letters and speeches during what was to be a spa retreat in Switzerland. During the summer of 1896, while on a cycling holiday in France (again, to improve their constitutions), they heard about the plight of the Armenian refugees streaming into Marseille from Armenia and immediately diverted there.

When Lady Henry and Frances Willard reached Marseille in mid-September 1896, they quickly assessed the situation to determine the refugees' immediate needs. They found an unused hospital ward in a monastery and convinced the local authorities to let them use it rent-free, to house and feed three hundred people—mostly funded by Lady Henry. They sent letters to contacts in Britain and the US, asking for donations. Lady Henry sent a telegram to J. D. Rockefeller, who responded by sending one thousand dollars. They sent some of the Armenians to contacts in the US, while some went to Lady Henry's property at Reigate Priory. Each person received the cost of their passage and the necessary minimal funds to satisfy immigration rules in each country. Donations helped to defray all these costs while much was paid by Lady Henry's personal finances.

KBF likely received an introduction to Lady Henry and Frances Willard in Marseille through her connection with James Rendel Harris, whom author Alessandro Falcetta, in a 2018 biography, describes as "Bible and patristic scholar, manuscript collector, Quaker theologian, devotional writer, traveller, folklorist, and relief worker." Lady Henry, Rendel Harris, the Duke of Westminster (Hugh Grosvenor), and several others established the Friends of Armenia in 1897, after Harris and his wife, Helen Balkwill Harris, had visited Asia Minor on a fact-finding mission in March 1896. Through these channels and common acquaintances among the missionaries they knew, KBF became connected with Harris and Balkwill Harris, corresponding with both of them in the autumn of 1896 and through 1897.

KBF was fluent in Armenian and had a strong command of French. Not being of independent means, KBF sought assistance to raise the necessary fare to Marseille. James L. Barton of the American Board appealed to the generosity of the Harrises, who readily paid KBF's passage.

On arriving in Marseille in September 1896, KBF took a modest room at 6 Boulevard de Notre Dame, within walking distance of the port. She wrote from there to Rendel Harris that she found Lady Henry and Frances Willard to be "the nicest people in the world." The feeling seems to have been mutual. Perhaps knowing of KBF's limited means, Lady Henry paid for her room. And Frances Willard, soon to celebrate her fifty-seventh birthday, expressed gratitude in her journal for both KBF's capabilities and willingness to pitch in: "[The refugees] are now altogether comfortable—food cooked by Armenians and to their liking, savory and oniony and taken squatting! Miss Frazer [*sic*] is doing well—getting all their names, histories, etc. She was in Van all last winter through the massacres with Dr. Kimball and solaces them more than anyone."

Initially, through the rest of September and the first part of October, the work of processing refugees in Marseille barely left KBF time to eat or sleep, and Frances Willard noted that KBF and Lady Henry were "all day at the refuge." KBF's first letters from Marseille still in existence date from mid-October 1896, after Lady Henry and Frances Willard returned to London. By then, KBF was becoming more confident in and assertive about her capabilities, even if expressed within the bounds of what was socially acceptable for a twenty-nine-year-old lady of the time. Sensibilities required well-mannered young women not to speak up about their capabilities, to demur or deflect whenever anyone else spoke about them, and to defer to men and older women whenever necessary—qualities with which KBF sometimes struggled.

By September 1896, KBF was no longer the naive young woman who travelled to Armenia with firm ideas about what to think and do, based on limited experience and second-hand opinions. Dr. Grace Kimball's example was a tremendous influence on her. This, coupled with her own experiences, gave KBF more confidence. Doubtless her brief but intense experience with Lady Henry and Frances Willard—who never shied from speaking their minds—added to her self-possession. (Writing years later about the sort of staff she would not hire to work in her centre, Lady Henry said she didn't want "the clever, the self-confident, the up-to-date woman with her ready-made classifications of human beings and her fixed notions of success and failure," all of which could have described KBF when she first embarked for Armenia.)

Though "very glad" to have gone to Marseille, "for I think I was really useful as long as Lady Henry and Miss Willard remained," KBF was "feeling these last few days as if I might as well be somewhere else." The source of irritation was the fact that while she was fluent in the Armenian language, a Salvation Army officer and manager of the Social Department, Col. Stitt, to whom she had been assigned to help, far preferred a male translator who, in her opinion, "doesn't know very good English and his French is not much better." She attempted to soften her criticism by adding "so mistakes are sometimes made but not such very bad ones. The Colonel really does very well." She further added: "The Salvation Army certainly is doing excellent work in receiving & caring for some of those who arrive in New York. I must remember to tell Col. Stitt about the telegram & how much everyone appreciates the work of the army."

KBF's frustration at these small dismissals is thinly veiled in some of her letters. In one to her mentor and benefactor Professor Harris, dated October 11, 1896, she wrote: "To tell you the truth Prof Harris I have not had the spirit of love for my co-workers this week that perhaps I ought to have had, but I am going to do better tomorrow. I've really not been very naughty outwardly but quite impatient enough."

One can imagine what it must have been like to know one's capabilities and wish to employ them in meaningful activities while society restricted a woman's ability to show her mettle or even articulate clearly frustration with men's control over so many aspects of the relief work. No doubt KBF found both a sympathetic ear and strong encouragement from Lady Henry and Frances Willard.

Her flashes of irritation conveyed in correspondence were doubtless at having her abilities dismissed or ignored because she was a woman but were also fed by her impatience to return to Van. According to sources within the Armenian community in Marseille, another attack by the Revolutionists in Constantinople was imminent, making it unsafe for her to return there. She wrote to mission agencies in Boston and Constantinople, sharing the intelligence, saying that she was prepared to go "as it suits them," and asking whether she should await word in Marseille or in England. She felt certain that her services were no longer required in Marseille, and if Constantinople wasn't an option, then she wished to help the efforts in Bulgaria.

Bulgaria was exceptional among European countries in that the country willingly opened its borders to the refugees, having itself experienced massacres all too recently. Bulgaria's means were severely limited, however, and it looked to international aid such as that provided by missionary agencies to assist with the huge influx of mouths to feed and bodies to clothe and house.

Still treading the delicate balance of ladylike propriety, in a letter to Professor Harris dated October 18, KBF highlighted her eagerness and downplayed her frustration by asking, "I am sure I should like any one whom you would send with me, but ought I not be brave enough to go alone? Or would you fear that I should get lost?... If you get answer from [the Board], wire me at once and I shall start immediately in whichever direction you name." A few lines later she attempted to smooth the way even further. Even then, she was indignant at a slight to Lady Henry.

> You will be glad...to know that last week was a really happy one because I did not allow little things to worry me as I did the former week. My impatience tho' was not on my account alone. It provoked me for the Salvation Army people to be continually asserting their great necessity to the cause and saying that Lady Henry could not have got along without them. Perhaps she

could not have had the people met at Paris and London but in Marseille decidedly she could have dispensed with them. Today's 'Lines' speaks as if it was the Army that sent all the Armenians to America and as a matter of fact, Col. Stitt had almost nothing to do with their being sent. Lady Henry made all the arrangements herself and paid for each ticket herself.... When will there be peace and safety in Turkey? Even without it, I long to go back to my people in Van. How I wish they would let me go. However, I am ready to go anywhere else I can do good.

Chapter Ten

"Somehow the misery of it all seems greater to me... perhaps because I have less power to help"

At some point after her October 18 letter to Professor Harris, KBF travelled to Budapest where she wrote to him on October 30. She expressed confusion about arrangements to meet up with a Mrs. Allen (not the wife of the missionary Rev. Allen whom she knew from Van). The tone of the letter borders on panic as she wondered where a miscommunication occurred. Was she to meet Mrs. Allen in Munich or Vienna? Train timetables confused her further, and she felt she had no other option than to book a ticket on the Orient Express for Budapest, where she knew Mrs. Allen planned to stop. KBF apologized for the extra expense of taxis, hotel, and a seat on the Orient Express, but having no one else to consult, she made her way as best she could. Happily, Mrs. Allen turned up as expected and told KBF that the refugees flooding into Varna, Bulgaria, needed her help.

Consequently, Mrs. Allen and KBF travelled together to Bulgaria at the beginning of November 1896, stopping in Philippopolis. Now known as Plovdiv, the city is one of the oldest in Europe, named in 342 BC for the man who conquered it: Philip II of Macedon, father of Alexander the Great. Its roots, however, run even deeper with archaeological remains dating it to a much earlier time.

KBF took a room the Hotel Feller, and Mrs. Allen stayed at the home of a Russian pastor, Mr. Tonjoroff, and his wife. Based on first-hand accounts reported by Reuters, which identified Bourgas and Varna as areas of greatest need for refugees, Mrs. Tonjoroff and Mrs. Allen planned to travel to Bourgas, the second largest city in Bulgaria. KBF, however, wanted to go to Varna, where she knew "two very nice Armenian families...and it would be easier for me to be there alone than in Bourgas, at least I think so." To that end, KBF travelled to Bourgas with Mrs. Allen and Mrs. Tonjoroff to await a boat to take her to Varna.

All KBF's plans—from how she travelled, to where she stayed, to the activities in which she engaged to carry out relief—relied on financial assistance from several sources. Her personal income did not allow her to travel without careful planning or even to determine entirely her plans to supervise relief efforts. Some of her funds came from the Congregational Church's American Board of Commissions for Foreign Missions, of which she was a member. She was always on the lookout for other sources, having experienced first-hand while in Turkey the catastrophic consequences if one source dried up.

In a letter to James Rendel Harris, KBF confided that a rift had developed among agencies providing relief. Some funds came from the US, some from the UK and Russia. As wife of a Russian pastor, Mrs. Tonjoroff had power and influence and regarded KBF with some suspicion because KBF belonged to the American Board. According to KBF, Mrs. Tonjoroff, the "[d]ear old lady,"

> [thinks] she is the right one to help and advise Mrs. Allen in all things.... Mrs. Tonjoroff has been exceedingly kind and lovely but there is a little something that we all feel. Now naturally it is right for Mrs. Allen to lean on Mrs. Tonjoroff and to work together, but three heads are too many, and as you were good enough to trust me with some money, I feel that I ought to be the one to spend it. Therefore to avert any possible friction would it not be better for them to go to Bourgas and me to go to Varna?... Believe me, Prof. Harris, I am praying to be guided aright in all things and feeling my own weakness. I am leaning on a strong arm. I do want to do the right and best thing always.

KBF's diplomatic choice of words was a thin veneer over the fact that, based on her four years in Van, she felt herself capable of taking responsibility for providing relief to Armenian refugees. She chafed at the supervision of Mrs. Tonjoroff in their activities and perhaps also at the deferral of Mrs. Allen to Mrs. Tonjoroff's opinions.

Clearly, KBF wished to run the show in Varna, both because she believed herself capable of doing so and to show her elders that regardless of her age she was perfectly qualified. By mid-November, under the direction of Charles Brophy of the Westminster Committee, she got more than her wish: responsibility for organizing relief for 6,100 refugees in that city, 610 in Shumla (modern-day Shumen), 84 in Pravady (modern-day

Provadia), 130 in Dobrich, and 233 in Silistria (modern-day Silistra). A quick glance at a map shows that both Provadia and Dobrich are located approximately 50 kilometres away from Varna, Shumen almost 90, and Silistra on the border of Romania about 150 kilometres away—considerable distances to travel in 1897. KBF knew she would have to find people whom she could trust to carry out orders and keep her apprised of developments. This effort proved somewhat frustrating.

In a letter to her cousin Sadie in November 1896 she wrote:

> Today, I feel we did something. So many sick and absolutely penniless families were relieved. I am profiting by my knowledge of Dr. Kimball's work last year. I am always asking myself what would she do in such and such a place. There are some good men on the Armenian committee here but their slowness drives me wild. The other day I sent up for two good, responsible men. That would take time, they would have to meet, etc., etc., Well, I waited one day. On the second they hadn't arrived, and I selected my own men. On the third, about 3 P.M., their two arrived. I never can get an answer from them inside of three hours when I send up a message. Consequently, I do not send very often.

She needed "responsible men" to help carry out the work in centres located over a considerable geographic distance from her headquarters in Varna, men whom she could trust implicitly with finances and work details, including shipping items produced by refugees in "industrial relief" workshops via a company in Hamburg through agents in London. In her correspondence, she refers by surnames only to several "responsible men" whom she entrusted: Barons Kerafor, Katchadoorian, Findjandjian, Ovaghinian, and Neshan.

Initially, the greatest focus of relief work was in recording and assessing all who applied for relief. Funds paid for rent "if the family cannot possibly afford to do so." And if the family could afford rent, relief funds paid for "fuel and food," consisting of bread rations for all, and soup for some, though "[most] manage to scrape [money] together and buy their own meat." She estimated that she spent "900 francs a day, at a rate of 15 centimes per head." Despite the large numbers of people, KBF and her team of "responsible men" kept a close eye on everyone on the relief list. If a person was deemed fit to work but either refused to work or wasn't looking for work, their rations were cut in half. On one occasion, when KBF had a gut feeling that one fellow wasn't truthful about his circumstances, she had one of her "responsible men" follow him—right to a gambling establishment. She summoned the man and promptly cut off his funds.

As she said in her letter to Sadie, in her efforts, KBF had the excellent example of the aid set up by Grace Kimball. Indeed, after she left the country, she wrote, "insofar as my work...in Bulgaria was successful, it was in a large measure due to the observation of [Kimball's] methods in Van." Within the first few days of arriving in Varna, and with some assistance from the mayor, Mr. Zheko Zhekov, KBF toured facilities set aside for refugees by the Bulgarian government and began to meet with those applying for relief, taking extensive histories on each person. The Bulgarian government housed eight hundred people in a former hospital and another six thousand in cottages, "one family to a room, sometimes two if the room is a large one." Even so, KBF described that many desperate people were "packed like sardines" in some accommodations, giving rise to concerns about the outbreak and spread of disease.

> When people arrived from Constantinople they sold extra furniture and bedding—those that had any—and rented houses, some for one month, others for two and three, some even for six months. Afterwards they sold every little thing possible to buy bread, in some cases even the shoes off their children's feet—and so they have been living. Now everything is sold, the rent is due and they are desperate. I seem to have arrived in the nick of time and it isn't wonderful that they consider me an angel. The rent is going to be a big item in the expenses.... A good many of the cottages will be uninhabitable in the winter. I am sending out men tomorrow to make lists of the families in the very worst houses. They, together with many whose rent has expired I think we will send to Shumleh, where large houses can be rented at a low price.... The government sends the refugees over its railways free and we shall only have to pay for the transportation of their few belongings to the station. It will be much cheaper to keep them in Shumleh than here.

In her first week, KBF personally examined the circumstances of seven hundred families and felt overwhelmed by their pitiful tales of suffering. Many, she knew, had lived "from hand to mouth all their lives" and therefore did not suffer as much as those who "a few months ago had everything and now are penniless." She wrote, "A man came to me yesterday with cold perspiration dripping from his pale face. Trembling all over and in a shaking voice, begged help for his wife and three children who were all in bed together, sick. A few weeks ago, he owned two shops in Constantinople, has now outstanding debts of £2000 due him and he is starving."

Writing after her time in Bulgaria, KBF painted a picture of the state of things when she first arrived and the scope of the work she did to address the dire circumstances of the refugees.

> Fourteen thousand landed in Varna, a city of 35,000, causing serious congestion. The authorities were alarmed, and gave 4000 or more free transportation into the interior towns. On arriving in Varna, I found 150 people living in quarantine buildings across the harbour and 800 in the old hospital, in the south end of the town, which had been placed at their disposal by the municipality. The others were scattered about the town, some in small huts and cottages, packed like sardines in a box, and still others comfortably settled in good homes, for about 2000 refugees were able to provide for themselves. Many of these people were absolutely destitute when they landed, others had brought a few things with them, which they had sold to pay for a roof under which to sleep, for many of the householders refused to take them into their homes until rent had been paid in advance.
>
> Many had sold even their beds to pay rent and they were selling clothes from off their backs and even the shoes from tiny infant feet to buy bread to keep body and soul together. The Varna Armenians had formed a committee which had collected funds for supplying the quarantine and hospitals with daily rations of bread, but the thousands outside had nothing and starvation was written in their faces. The morning after my arrival I visited the English Consul, who asked me to take charge of the disbursement of the large sums of money which were to come from the Duke of Westminster's

fund. So I was enabled to organize relief on a larger scale than I had anticipated, in fact to prepare to take charge for the winter of all the needy refugees in Varna and of the adjacent small towns. The former committee was comprised of business men too busy to give their whole time to relief work. It was amusing to see how readily they turned all the responsibility for their people over to me. Although they were never willing to take the initiative they always very gladly helped me when called upon to do so.

We worked together in perfect harmony. I found the three men whom they had put in charge of the hospital very excellent fellows, and using the hospital as the central office I began work with them. The refugees outside received our first attention. Notice was given that one member from each family should come to the hospital at once to register. But they came in crowds, mothers, sisters, cousins and brothers. I personally inquired into the case of each family, secretaries taking down the parents' names, number of children, trade (if any), present condition and probable need during the winter. All their statements were later verified by examiners sent to their dwelling places.

To summarize briefly the winter's work, over 8000 people were cared for. The funds at my disposal amounted to $75,000 [approximately US$2 million today], mostly from England from the Duke of Westminster's fund, Prof. Rendel Harris and the Society of Friends. Smaller sums also came from Germany and Switzerland. In the spring 200 families were returned to Constantinople, others have since

> gone, but 3000 remain in Varna who will need help this winter. All honor and praise is due the Bulgarians who remembering what they had suffered under the heel of the oppressor, opened their doors and welcomed these persecuted people to whom their neighbours refused entrance. The government gave free doctors and medicine, free railway transportation from Varna. It contemplated a gift of land to encourage organization, but when the list of trades was made out, it was found that agriculturists were too few to warrant that scheme. The Mayor of Varna, Mr. [Zhekov], a graduate of Robert College, cannot be praised too highly for his interest in the suffering people.

Missing from this text, presented at the thirteenth annual Woman's Board of Missions meeting in New London, Connecticut, in November 1898, are details of events that tried KBF's patience in the extreme, sometimes tipping her over the edge into rage.

The British social reformer, women's rights advocate, and writer Laura Ormiston Dibbin Chant visited Varna in December 1897 and penned an article that included a glowing report of KBF's work. Though KBF kept the clipping in her journal, it made a suggestion that affronted KBF, treading (as she felt it did) on her ability to make decisions, to prioritize and to organize.

> It is a heroic spectacle, that of a young and bright woman supporting on her shoulders the weight of such a stupendous work as superintending the housing, feeding, clothing and a hundred other cares of a family of over 5000 people, and though much more than this

needs to be done if these fugitives are not to be wholly pauperized, to this one painstaking, self-sacrificing little woman belongs the credit of a most excellent administration of the larger funds sent out to her from England and America, and of having most creditably broken the neck of the earlier strain on the resources of a comparatively small town like Varna. Much still needs to be done that Miss Fraser can not do, and that ought to be taken in hand at once by some organization of a different nature and constitution different from that which she at present represents, namely the Duke of Westminster's and Prof. Rendall Harris' funds, and it is to be hoped that while on the one hand due recognition is most generously given of the important work that has been accomplished by those funds through which Miss Fraser is actually snatching thousands of people from the imminent perils of starvation and death from exposure, the more permanent organization shall bear in mind that many of these refugees are men who have owned large mercantile establishments, professional men of good standing, women who have been delicately reared, and children belonging to well-to-do classes for whom a place like Varna offers no opening; and that to provide means for their fresh start in places where there is a demand for extended industries and professional services, is the most economical as well as the wisest way in the long run of relieving their present distress.... Also, a thoroughly efficient school for both boys and girls, including compulsory training in the use of the gymnasium and bath room, presents one solution of the difficult problem of the future of children whose early years have been so heavily handicapped. Surely in gratitude for the disinterested hospitality of Bulgaria in taking this tremendous human immigration so kindly and with such genuine solicitude to meet the emergency, the rest of the world should generously aid in contributing to the permanent relief of persecuted and tortured Armenia. But yesterday I stood in a tiny room, seven feet high and seven by seven, and in my hands held in pitying tenderness those of an Armenian lady whose three sons and husband were massacred before her eyes. Angels must surely weep over grief such as hers. What tears must be given by a loving wife and mother from a happy home. She is receiving bread from the hospital; but that is small comfort for one whose nerves give answer to the awful demands made on them in acute and constant neuralgia. Varna does not promise much in the way of means to earn a livelihood for her, and scores of others who have all been shipwrecked in the same storm. Who shall think out wisely and with the golden rule before them the plan of deliverance for these? But apart from all devices for relief is there no brain, no heart in all the governments of the world that all together or in groups they can not say to the Sultan of Turkey: "We will not permit you to deprive this ancient people of its heritage; you shall in the name of our common humanity allow these exiles to return their home places; you shall enter into such guarantees for their rights of citizenship as shall at least place their safety and freedom on the same level as that of the Turkish nation of which they are politically a part. The common rights of man demand it. Justice, mercy and common sense demand it. The common safety of

> Europe and the future progress of the world demand it. It must therefore be done; we call on you to do it; will you do it, or—?" And it is with the hope of an international association being able to influence such a consummation, as well as collect and diffuse reliable information as to what is being done and the needs as they arise, that the scheme with which Lady Henry Somerset and Miss Frances E. Willard are so closely connected seems to my mind to be the necessary corollary of all relief funds and local organizations.

Shortly after the article appeared, KBF learned that Lady Henry took the recommendations to heart. No longer content simply to provide funds for relief efforts, she intended to have a say in Varna activities—all the way from London. Gratitude for Lady Henry's generosity, and happiness for the warm relationship KBF developed with both Lady Henry and Frances Willard, became "dismay and sorrow" when Lady Henry decided to send her own contingent from the UK to help with the relief operations.

KBF was confident in her assessment of people to discern those deserving of aid from those who knew how to take advantage of a system. Even after spending so much time amongst Armenians, KBF remained class conscious and wary of becoming associated with extremist groups, noting in one letter that she was delayed in replying because "four Armenians wasted my precious time. I couldn't tell them to go as they weren't of the begging class, but I can keep them out another time for I imagine they belong to the Revolutionists."

Upon learning of Lady Henry's plans to send those she handpicked to assist in relief efforts (among them Laura Ormiston Dibbin Chant), KBF wrote her to say: "[I]t is a very great pity to send so many people out here. With so many heads some one will be sure to get badly cheated. I have already had more than twelve applications for help from people who are distinctly cheats. Those who are really honest among the refugees will be tempted to try and get a share in the riches which, to them, appears to come so freely from England."

Complaining to Professor Harris, KBF wrote:

> For the friends which you are sending it is different. They will I am sure be willing to listen at least to suggestions. But Mrs. Chant and Mrs. Kritchian are different people. Fancy sending an Armenian out on such an errand, especially a Revolutionist! Will you please tell me what the rumour was about me? It must have been something to cause Lady Henry to lose her trust in me, otherwise I was on the spot. I should think that she would have asked me about the state of things here. We are expecting Sir Arthur and Lady [Henrietta] Hayter, and Major [illegible] this evening. They come to look into the work with the idea of establishing an agricultural colony in Bulgaria. Fancy how important the Armenians will feel, those three people coming, then your three friends, and lastly Lady Henry's contingent. However all but the last three will work in unison and perhaps they, too, will be good and sensible. I have asked Lady Henry what she thinks about sending her friends to Rouschuk as there are about 2000 refugees there.

KBF's challenges and frustrations did not end with those who provided funds for relief work. She also had to contend with Bulgarian government officials and Armenian elders who were prepared to ignore any orders or refuse to comply with any requests made by a woman—especially a young, diminutive one. Initially KBF was infuriated. Eventually, however, she learned to circumvent, sidestep, or sweet-talk those who got in her way and to ignore anyone whom she could not ultimately convince. There were a couple of occasions, as donations dried up and funds to purchase supplies dwindled, when she stood her ground in the face of verbal abuse and threats of physical assault, gaining the respect of at least some of the men who initially tried to overrule her.

Her friendship with a Mr. Adams, a Quaker engaged in relief work, provided her with a sympathetic ear and the encouragement to get through times when she either felt she couldn't go on or wanted to give up in frustration. As part of KBF's relief operations, Adams established "industrial relief" workshops in Varna and Shumla, employing one hundred men—"carpenters, blacksmiths, coppersmiths, carers and hammock makers"—making furniture, housewares, and hammocks to be sold locally and in the UK to raise funds for relief work. In the letters KBF exchanged with Adams during her sojourn in Bulgaria, she shared his frustration over bureaucratic interference and expressed herself so candidly that he dubbed her "The Autocrat."

Based on her several years' experience pleading for funds from various organizations; writing thank-you letters that she often felt were obsequious and used up time that could be put to better use; and enduring what she deemed interference by those who, though well-intentioned, lacked her first-hand experience, she found the Quakers' approach, as exemplified by Mr. Adams and the Harrises with their Friends of Armenia group, simple and refreshing. "[The next donation] shall be written in big letters as from the Friends next time. It's so good to have the strong support of the Friends. They are the best possible friends to have and after this I shall always feel that success is assured if I undertake to do anything with your Society as backers."

After Adams met Mrs. Tonjoroff, KBF wrote him: "Do you think that I was not far wrong in what I said about Mrs. Tonjoroff? Dear me, I would not work in the same city with her for a good deal. I mean in the same branch of work." She commiserated with him about their shared frustration with some of those whom they encountered in the work—Armenian and non-Armenian alike. And she appreciated Adams's ability to smooth her way with some government officials. For the most part, though, she took command, confronting overt snubs of her authority and passive-aggressive responses to requests she made.

While Adams's workshops turned out iron bedsteads, wooden cabinets, tables, and chairs, KBF used relief funds to purchase cloth and leather that could be used by tailors, dressmakers, and cobblers who could be found "in abundance [and who were] crying for work." Further, many of the women practised a fine embroidery unique to Armenian culture, with variations that distinguished work of one community from another. KBF employed "90 women and girls...earning a franc a day." The first month's proceeds from the women's needlework provided £92, with which KBF helped some refugees start businesses by purchasing tools and "material to work with."

KBF used some of the relief funds to organize a school with "bright and pretty" rooms in the former hospital. Initially built for the children residing at that site, requests to take pupils from the general refugee population in Varna led her to enlarge the school. By February 1897 there were 170 pupils on the roster. And when the municipality learned of this, they told her to refuse to permit "outsiders" in the hospital site school. She ignored their demand.

Soliciting funds and managing them to make them last as long as possible was a constant concern for KBF. Human suffering is never restricted to one place at a time on the planet, and causes are always in competition with one another for limited funds. In 1897, the plight of Armenians was only one story in the international media. Droughts in India in 1896 brought famine and disease to that country in 1897. KBF knew that when the world's focus turned to a new disaster in another place, funds would be diverted away from Armenian relief. That was trying enough, but providing relief through a cold winter compounded the stress. As funds dwindled, KBF was "considerably troubled to make both ends meet." Writing to Sadie, she said, "Sometimes when I awake in the morning, I dread to get up because I know there will be so many pleas, so much distress which I cannot help. However, I do feel that the people have been carried comfortably through the winter and now if their gloves are worn out, it is warmer weather."

Some who received help didn't feel complete gratitude, however. When KBF cut the expenses of some of the single men whom she felt could find work and better fend for themselves than those with families to support, a number of them objected by banding together to confront her, demanding that she restore their funds. Though somewhat unnerved by the "nasty looking set," she stood her ground and refused. They went away but returned in the afternoon to demand that she give them food three times a week. She refused and summoned two gendarmes. The group left again. KBF was stunned when two of the group's leaders returned a short time later to apologize for their actions. Afterwards, she reflected, "I have some rough times occasionally for there are villains among the refugees but so far I have come out ahead and mean to do so to the end."

For the most part people expressed "a great deal of thanks and gratitude," which she felt "didn't belong to your humble servant, as the money wasn't mine.... [Though] there are some ungrateful wretches, there are many very sincerely thankful people in this city of Varna today."

Money trickled in but did not keep up with expenditures. In February 1897, KBF travelled to Shumla with Mr. Ovaghinian where "[Baron] Neshan has been doing excellent work and for his pains had got himself disliked by one or two plotting men." After reviewing the accounts which were "done methodically and well," they jointly decided their only recourse was to cut rations and halt some of the work where the cost of doing so exceeded a reasonable return. Word spread quickly, even before KBF, accompanied by two of her "responsible men," Ovaghinian and Neshan, arrived at the church where refugees gathered to hear the unwelcome news.

Although most "received the cut in their rations very quietly," one woman stood up in the crowd to ask KBF aggressively what she planned to do about it. KBF replied that she could not give what she did not have, at which point the woman

> blazed forth, calling me all the vile names she could possibly think of. I grew half sick for a second for it was something new to me to be reviled in such a way. [When none of the men offered to interfere]...I ordered the gendarme to put her out. She threw him off like a feather. When I stepped in and sent for a second gendarme, Neshan whispered to me that she was connected with the Tashnagists and had come in to raise a row on their behalf. I asked those around if they weren't ashamed of themselves to stand quietly by and listen to that woman screaming at such a rate. By

> that time the second gendarme arrived and would you believe it, the two of them together couldn't manage her! But some of the roughs were coming to their senses and several men came and got her away.

With the woman's removal, the gathering calmed down. KBF explained that she had to reduce expenses. Accordingly, rations of soup and wood would be cut off for all men in Shumla while women and children would continue to receive the same as before. All would continue to receive bread rations and would have to fend for themselves for everything else. Apparently everyone agreed that hers was a difficult position and that nothing else could be done until the financial situation improved. But as she prepared to leave the church to return to her hotel, word came that several young men had gathered outside to demand the removal of Neshan and restoration of funds. She reasoned with them, appealing to them as "men of sense and good feeling," asking whether their consciences would permit them to take food from the mouths of women and children and what little warmth relief funds could provide in a cold winter. Most relented but a few insisted that she restore rations to former levels or sign a paper that she had refused them all aid. She stood her ground and returned to her hotel.

A short time later, Neshan confided that he believed the cook who prepared soup rations for the refugees was among those who instigated the resistance to reduced rations, advising her that the man "could be very useful or very harmful" in helping them to quell further angry demonstrations. KBF visited the cook, "flattered him a bit," and consulted him about how he might extend the food dollars even further, "telling him that his honour as a cook demanded that he should help me out in my economy. He entered into the spirit of it."

Satisfied that Neshan would have no further troubles in Shumla, KBF and Mr. Ovaghinian returned to Varna, where she had to advise refugees there that their rations, too, would have to be cut in the same manner as those in Shumla. In Pravady, she issued orders that the funds expended for rents and wood in February to the eighty-four refugees there would have to cease until further notice, while bread (which was more expensive to produce in Pravady than in the other locations) would continue to be distributed in the same rations until further notice. In February, in a letter to her Quaker colleague Mr. Adams, KBF wrote in a weary tone: "I wish some wealthy old lady in England [perhaps she meant Lady Henry Somerset?] would take the responsibility of those 84 people upon her shoulders. She wouldn't miss 50 francs [per week]."

A donation of 300 francs from a Mr. Levoir in Marseille and another £500 from the Westminster Fund in February 1897 were welcome but not nearly enough. KBF was thankful for "a holy week" that, because the faithful had to fast, permitted her to restrict rations even further to "olive oil, beans, and bread."

Finding and managing funds to support relief work wasn't KBF's only financial concern. She received meagre subsistence wages for her work. Dr. Harris sent her £20 in November 1896—a generous sum for the day but hardly enough to keep her housed and fed all winter. Embarrassed to have to ask him directly for more, in mid-March she prevailed upon her friend Mr. Adams to intervene on her behalf without making it sound as though the request came directly from her.

The municipality created "more trouble than all the rest of my work" by sending inspectors to the hospital property in March 1897 and informing her that the facility housed too many people. "Only 450 could remain in the place." She scrambled to find places for a number of families, some of whom found work, while some returned to Constantinople. Within just over a week, she managed to reduce the number in the hospital facility from just over eight hundred to five hundred, hoping that the municipality would show some leniency in their numbers.

The inspectors turned their attention to the embroidery workshop, telling KBF that one of their doctors deemed the workroom to be too small for the one hundred workers employed and demanding that all work cease immediately. Although the hospital was packed, even after a few hundred people moved out, KBF freed up another space so that two rooms—one holding sixty, the other holding forty—could be dedicated to the embroidery work, which "are selling at double price in England" and providing a revenue stream essential to continuing relief work in Bulgaria.

KBF wrote to the municipality and to Sir Arthur Hayter (former finance secretary to the War Office and superintendent of the Duke of Westminster Fund) "that if the work is stopped, the municipality will have to look after the 90 families supported by the department.... [F]unds are coming in slowly, and by and by perhaps the refugees will again be thrown on the town." Regardless, the municipality insisted that the embroidery work cease immediately, the addition of a second room notwithstanding. They also threatened to close down the school altogether.

Mayor Zheko Zhekov, who had thus far been of great help to her, was away on other business during KBF's squabble with the municipality, and she hoped for his return in order to help sort out the situation. The vice mayor of Varna (whom KBF does not name) allied himself with one of the Armenian elders, a Mr. Hovasepian, who advised KBF that henceforth, any letters or requests concerning relief work or the premises in which they took place would have to pass Mr. Hovasepian's inspection and approval before being passed along to the municipality. KBF seethed, not just because two men tried to tell her how to do the work she already knew so well and was charged to carry out, but because such interference slowed down both the relief work and the industrial work that provided essential funds to sustain relief work.

Whenever KBF wrote letters in Armenian or French (both of which were spoken in Varna), the vice mayor or Mr. Hovasepian insisted they be translated into Bulgarian. In an attempt to placate the men, she complied by surrendering the letters for translation. But when the letters returned for her review before being submitted, Mr. Hovasepian told her to proofread the letters but not put her signature on them. His was all that was necessary. Annoyed, she not only proofread but edited the letters, adding comments pertaining to any work she carried out directly. "There was a nice chance for a row, but it did not seem necessary.... But in case of any trouble, [I knew they would respond with] 'It was Miss Fraser who did so-and-so.'"

Mr. Hovasepian insisted on being the first to examine all shipments of clothing destined for the refugees, "keeping back an occasional box of clothing, much to the disgust of his partner, and distributing them from his office. He tells me that they are worthless things, not fit to send to me. My men say differently." Though loyal to KBF, both Baron Findjandjian and Baron Katchadoorian felt great discomfort at the conflict between KBF, the vice mayor, and Mr. Hovasepian. KBF wrote to Mr. Adams, "I wish you could have seen the faces of Mr. Findjandjian and Mr. Katchadoorian when the message came that my signature was not necessary. I was very angry, but I had to laugh about them."

Mr. Zhekov returned to Varna ("such a relief to have him back") and after "a pleasant interview with the mayor...a load—such a heavy one—rolled away, away. He is a good fellow." Mayor Zhekov, Charles Brophy of the Westminster Fund, and a Mr. Konan intervened with the vice mayor and Mr. Hovasepian, calming the situation. Though KBF did not detail what transpired, the resolution was sufficient to move her to write that "Mr. Konan is a pretty good fellow and so is Mr. H. in his own way. We are good friends apparently, and I think we shall remain so."

Before the winter was out, KBF's trusted group of "responsible men" was reduced when Baron Kerafor fell gravely ill, and it rapidly became apparent that he would not recover.

> After church this P.M. I went to see Baron Kerafor.... He knows now that there is no hope for him and we talked for a while. He was muttering something when I went in, nobody could tell what. After I spoke to him, he said "I've been praying. Do you think Christ will forgive all my sins?" He seemed to put implicit trust in my answer and when I came away, he said that he was content and happy to go. I doubt if he lives through the night, poor fellow. He was so strong and well a few months ago. He, Baron Katchadoorian, and Findjandjian have been like three brothers this winter, true to breast as it was possible for one to be, and I know honest and faithful men. It pleased him this P.M. to be told what help he had been and how well he had done his work. Baron Katchadoorian is caring for him as if he were his dearest brother. Mr. Findjandjian is doing all he can, but he cannot stand the strain like Baron Katchadoorian.

In March 1897, money troubles were far from over. The Westminster Fund was about to dry up. Charles Brophy delivered the unhappy news that £1,000 "was their final limit. If it isn't one thing," KBF wrote, "it's another these days. However, I am getting used to it." Rations were again reduced in all refugee centres. KBF prayed for more funds to come from somewhere. She knew that some would come from the Society of Friends and from unnamed benefactors in Germany to get them through April, "however one doesn't know what may turn up" to upset the delicate financial balance.

By the end of March, with optimism that Lord Hayter, superintendant of the Westminster fund, could "use his influence in getting the Sultan bound to keep the peace," KBF wondered whether paying the fares of a few families who wished to return to Constantinople would be cheaper than keeping them on relief in Bulgaria. "They long to go but they are afraid, altho' many would go if they had money. They have houses there and will never be happy elsewhere."

Sometime that same month, she received the following letter from the Archibishop of the Armenian Church in Constantinople:

> MALACHIA SERVANT OF JESUS CHRIST BY THE MERCY OF GOD THE FATHER AND BY THE GRACE OF THE HOLY GHOST, AND BY THE WILL OF THE NATION, ARCHBISHOP OF CONSTANTINOPLE AND PATRIARCH OF THE ARMENIANS IN TURKEY.
>
> To kind and faithful Miss Katherine Fraser, Christ-given greetings and God-given blessings!
>
> With thankful heart we are informed that your kindness with tender mercy and care, since many years, has been

giving medical aid and necessities to the unfortunate refugees of our nationality in Varna and Shumla, through the donations of kind-hearted persons.

If, according to the word of our Lord, even a glass of cold water given to the disciples of the Gospel does not remain unrewarded, then there is no doubt that the kind of humanitarian work you have been doing for the poor, giving them food, clothing and relief, specially during this winter season, you are worthy of the blessings of our Lord Jesus Christ who writes unto his name all deeds of kindness.

Therefore, we who humbly supervise the Armenian Church in the confines of the Ottoman Empire, on behalf of our dear nation and in the name of the grateful refugees of Varna and Shumla, we thank you for them and we pray to God to bless you and those who trust you their cheerful offerings, and pray that God may keep you all free from all griefs and trials, and give you all long and prosperous lives.

Wishing you health and blessings from the Heavenly Father, and from us, Amen.

This letter of blessing was given on the 15th of the month of February, in the year 1897, with the Number 7.

(signed) ARCHBISHOP MALACHIA

Though too exhausted, frustrated, and frantic for funds to appreciate this gesture fully, she felt that "people here [in Bulgaria] are greatly pleased that the Patriarch has sent me this recognition of my winter's work here."

The timing of the Patriarch's greeting might have been influenced by reports sent him—possibly by KBF's "responsible men"—that a vartabed (priest) of the Armenian Church was using his pulpit to criticize what he deemed were miserly relief funds from England and to censure KBF for what he perceived as her lacklustre support of refugees in that city. KBF, who spoke Armenian fluently, attended a service and sat in silent, seething embarrassment at his tirade. She heard a mortified member of the congregation quietly ask a young woman in her company to take KBF from the church rather than suffer the attack. KBF, however, preferred to face down the vartabed. She remained in her seat. A short time later, "the preacher wandered a bit from his text" and the service continued. KBF did not, however, return to that church again. For their part, the congregation met with the vartabed after the incident and "invited" him to leave Varna a few days later.

At the end of March, KBF wrote her friend Elizabeth Huntingdon in Spain, telling her that Dr. Clarke, a physician serving on behalf of the American Board in Varna, was sufficiently concerned about KBF's health that he wrote a letter to the board to tell them KBF was in desperate need of a furlough. An earlier request by KBF, which does not appear in any surviving correspondence found thus far, was apparently ignored or refused, as KBF writes that through Dr. Clarke's intervention, "perhaps they will be easily persuaded this time."

In writing of the same situation in a letter to Mr. Adams, however, KBF took a different tone: "Dr. Clarke has the craziest scheme imaginable for me. He thinks that I am tired and ill and do not know it. He advises my going at once to a sanitorium at Clifton Springs, New York. Fancy what the American Board would say. If I could go so far, should I stop less than home? Such nonsense!"

In April, KBF wrote Sadie one Sunday that, after working until eight o'clock the night before, she went straight to bed without eating supper and on waking the next morning still felt utterly exhausted. She stayed in bed, "half up and half down," to catch up on correspondence. She confided, "The strain has been quite heavy this winter and I suppose I am feeling it a bit. I was thinking a little while ago how delightful it would be to be mothered a bit. I have had to think for so many people all winter that I should now be very happy if I could drop down in a spot where someone would do my thinking of a short time." In a letter dated about the same time, she wrote Mr. Adams: "Here is a queer request. Will you please ask Mrs. Adams if she knows anything to stop one's hair from coming out. I shall be bald very soon if I do not use something at once." Her descriptions of constant fatigue, muddled thinking, low mood, headaches, and hair loss raises the question of whether she had a medical condition such as a thyroid disorder or anemia. The symptoms are also consistent with slow poisoning caused by the iron, arsenic, and strychnine pills prescribed by Dr. Smith.

By May, the relief situation was desperate and tempers frayed. Lord and Lady Hayter, who had taken responsibility for refugee activity and relief work in Roustchouk (modern day Ruse, on the banks of the Danube), were unable to sustain activities there and wanted to move the refugees to Varna. KBF was frantic at the prospect, given that the situation for refugees in Varna was already severely strained. Adding more mouths to feed and bodies to clothe and house would break an already precarious situation. Once again, Mayor Zhekov came to her aid. Lord Hayter, without telling KBF, met with the mayor to appeal to him directly to accept more refugees. He refused.

Though relieved, KBF's relationship with Mr. Adams felt some strain because of the mayor's decision. Mr. Adams thought that sending refugees to Varna would boost production of fancy work and embroidery, which he sold to shops in the UK for a handsome price, thereby giving a boost to the revenue stream. Lady Hayter, even without moving refugees from Roustchouk to Varna, used her superior social standing to pull rank on KBF to commandeer some of the best needleworkers in the Varna workshop to meet "special orders for shopkeepers" to whom she provided goods. Chafing at these actions, KBF told Mr. Adams that she could not meet his orders and Lady Hayter's, too. Further, KBF informed Mr. Adams that she was mystified about Lady Hayter's demand when "she doesn't approve of this kind of oriental work. It offends her eyes."

What annoyed KBF wasn't only Lady Hayter overruling her, but the fact that middlemen engaged by Lady Hayter handled the goods, reaping "the profit of our hard work. [The girls who produce this work] ought to have a few more centimes per day. If an order is taken [through middlemen] it must be filled. If we lose, they lose." In contrast, any goods handled by Mr. Adams did not pass through any middlemen, and KBF preferred to keep things that way.

Her contretemps with Lady Hayter wasn't the only thing to preoccupy KBF at this time. Funds were so low that she cut off all relief efforts in Silistria, Dobritch, and Pravady, reducing her numbers by 2,300 refugees and leaving only the 4,000 in Shumla and Varna on her books. But even with that reduction, the lack of funds required KBF to cut rations once again. A few people banded together and persuaded "100 of the poorest and least sensible villagers" to give them their bread ration tickets, which a spokesman took to KBF's office. He demanded restoration of their former bread rations and handed KBF the tickets he collected, saying they would prefer a quick death than to starve to death slowly. Infuriated, she thanked him for return of the tickets and told him she would redistribute them to those who appreciated the help she could provide. Then she had the astonished man put out of the building and the gate locked behind him. She asked the police for two gendarmes to post at the gates in the event of reprisal.

Around six o'clock a messenger arrived with an unsigned letter from the group, telling her her life wouldn't be worth one *oke* (a small unit of measurement) and detailing consequences if she did not accede to their demands immediately. (No details exist in surviving letters.) She rounded on the messenger, icily telling him to carry her greetings back to the group and inform them she would not agree to their demands. She added that "If there should be any trouble, you will be the first one whom I shall give up to the gendarmes."

Early the next morning, a frantic worker arrived at her hotel, breathless, to tell her that a crowd had gathered at the hospital concerning a story about bread. He implored her to get there as soon as possible or there was "the likelihood of a big row." KBF sent the man to the police to dispatch gendarmes to the hospital. She hailed a carriage and rushed to the hospital, where she "found the gates closed and a very ugly looking crowd of men standing about."

Although they permitted her to pass by them and through the gates without interference, a few minutes after she arrived and began taking ration tickets in exchange for bread, a rock shattered an office window. "For a few seconds pandemonium reigned, women screamed, some fainted, others clutched my skirts." She tried to calm them, but a gendarme charged in the front door, sword drawn, thereby increasing the panicked confusion among a group of people who had witnessed massacres only a few short months before and giving KBF concerns it would all lead to a stampede. With relative calm quickly restored, KBF turned her attention to the noise outside.

She ran to the front gate, where she found five more gendarmes who asked her about the trouble. KBF filled them in while the hostile men who met her at the gate a short time before stood their ground. The gendarmes wanted to know the identities of the instigators. Fearing for the safety of men loyal to her should they identify any of them, she pointed out six including the messenger from the previous day whom she spied in the crowd. The gendarmes arrested the six and led them away, but the others remained, menacingly, by the front gate.

KBF returned to the hospital and encouraged the women who had received their bread rations to leave the building. They refused, afraid to pass by the men at the gate. KBF led them out to the gate, drawing herself up to her full five-foot-two-inches height, admonishing the men to let them pass. "I asked the men if it weren't enough that their women had been nearly frightened to death in Turkey, this morning you have acted so that your own wives and sisters are afraid to walk past you! Aren't you ashamed of yourselves? Some of them had the grace to say, 'Yes, it is a shame.'" But others remained at the gate, demanding that she tell the police to release the six arrested.

Infuriated, she told them there was nothing she could do, warning them, "If you don't leave this quarter at once I'll have every one of you arrested." She initially felt little remorse upon learning later that those arrested "were beaten in prison, not a nice mode of punishment" but felt more compassion when she was told that one required hospitalization after "a little bit too much" of a beating simply for stealing a gendarme's whistle in the fracas.

Upon their release, the victims sent a telegram to the government capital in Sophia, complaining of their "illegal mode of punishment" (whipping by police was not permitted). A short time later, KBF received a telegram from the government, demanding that she explain her role in the men's arrests and punishment. She sat up "half the night" composing a letter to her ally, Mayor Zhekov, asking him to help her explain the incident, concerned as she was that an unintended consequence of the event might be expulsion of all Armenians from Bulgaria. In the end, the men responsible for the incident were ordered to "scatter themselves within 15 days." When they failed to comply, the government rounded them up and expelled them from Bulgaria. Before leaving, the guilty tried to blame KBF for their fate, but she was confident that "there are many sensible Armenians who know that it was the wisest possible step to take."

KBF hoped that making an example of agitators would help to calm things and permit the necessary work to be carried out. But she was under no illusion that the relative quiet would continue indefinitely. The refugees' situation grew increasingly straitened as resources at KBF's disposal dwindled rapidly. KBF's steely resolve, however, did not harden her to suffering, as the need for help remained steady.

> Miss Long [one of KBF's assistants] sent me down another family tonight. I thought I had got so stony hearted that nothing would move me, but the poor creature who came this evening to my room was in such a plight that the hardest heart would have been touched. She is so delicate, and goes out of her mind occasionally, but was all right this evening. Her clothes were very thin and in poor condition. She had no stockings and I thought no shoes, but when I offered her my boots of rubber to wear down to the Hospital, she said that she had a pair of soles outside—her

husband was waiting for her outside. I gave her a letter [of introduction] to Mr. Findjandjian, asking him to put the family up for the night in as comfortable a place as possible. Somehow the misery of it all seems greater to me these few days than ever before, perhaps because I have less power to help. After writing my letters I am going to read my chapter aloud and imagine that I am not alone.

Where once KBF would have objected to suggestions that she needed a furlough, her increasing exhaustion is evident in her letters, in references to her irritability and her hair loss. KBF must have realized that beyond her desire to see her family and friends in North America, she really needed a break from the work. It certainly couldn't have helped that, given her clear ability to accept responsibility and deliver on expectations, she continued to be regarded by many as a mere girl. Having to justify one's abilities is, in itself, exhausting, without the added responsibility of caring for thousands of other people.

EPILOGUE

"Doing a man's work with more than a man's capability"

BECAUSE OF THE INCIDENT AT THE HOSPITAL AND THE SUBSEQUENT expulsion of the perpetrators, the chief of police posted gendarmes to keep watch over the premises to ensure no further problems. For her part, KBF felt there would not be another such outburst. In the delicate peace, however, she prepared to defend herself if necessary. "My office looks quite like my room in Van during the [siege] week, with rifles and bayonets in the corner."

Several letters from this time (May–June 1897) indicate that KBF's departure from Bulgaria was quickly approaching. She advocated strongly on behalf of two women who worked with her—Miss Long and Miss Droohe—to be her replacements. They worked well, maintained detailed records and accounts, and prepared regular reports essential to keeping the relief work moving as smoothly as possible despite funds that were unpredictable and could not be depended upon to

Four Armenian women at a rescue home after having been enslaved, c. 1921.
(WIKIMEDIA COMMONS)

arrive regularly. Some male names were also suggested, but she dismissed them as being not as well-prepared or experienced as the two women she recommended.

On May 31, 1897, KBF was delighted to receive in the mail a cheque for £600 from Mr. Adams—and equally devastated to receive a telegram on the same day telling her not to cash it. She sat down to write him a letter, describing the circumstances facing her. She needed bread for one or two months for one hundred families "who will actually starve if not helped." She told him that she had cut off from relief nearly three thousand people the previous day and urged him to "advance quickly the money paid out for industries. What I have will finish relief. If you were here just now, you would realize how difficult it is to refuse to help. I have to shut my eyes to a great deal of misery and shall have to close them very tight to steel my heart this week."

Even before she posted the letter, she received another telegram from Mr. Adams, at four thirty A.M. on June 1, advising her she could cash the cheque. Despite her relief, she had to tell the six hundred remaining refugees in her care that relief funds had all but come to an end. "Poor wretches, they are perfectly helpless people and I cannot see what they are going to do. The white faces of the multitude haunt me these days. During the last month and a half they have not had rent. The money which they could earn went to pay the landlord instead of to provide a little meat, therefore the colours of most of the women and children and many of the men, is bad to a degree."

She told them their bread rations would come to an end that Saturday, but "I shall have to help them in some way, otherwise there certainly will be deaths from hunger. There's quite a little sickness these days caused, I should say, from lack of nourishment." She anticipated that goods produced by the industries forwarded recently to Mr. Adams for sale in the UK would provide another £600, about half of which she wished to use to help the most sick and desperate left in her care. She apologized to Mr. Adams in advance if she spent more than he wished, but she felt she had no alternative.

The flow of surviving letters to her family and to Mr. Adams stopped abruptly after the second week of June 1897 and never really resumed. KBF's movements are unknown, though in one of her last letters she wrote that she had funds in the form of an unused ticket to travel as far as England, but not to Canada. When she left, she took a silver tea service presented to her by Mayor Zheko Zhekov as a token of the city of Varna's gratitude for her excellent work.

Scant details of her final two years can be found only in the obituaries published in the *Halifax Chronicle* and the *Yarmouth Herald*. Dr. Clarke's assessment in Varna that KBF was sicker than she knew, almost completely exhausted and in need of complete rest, led to her being granted a year-long furlough from relief work by the American Board. Somehow, she found passage to Canada.

During her year of rest, she managed to travel a few times to Yarmouth and to Boston to speak about the Armenians' need for aid and assistance. Her talks kept details of her involvement to a minimum, as modesty and decorum required.

On November 4, 1898, she addressed the Woman's Board of Missions in New London, Connecticut. In her concluding remarks she said: "When an Armenian comes to this country and you find him not all that you had imagined, please remember that for centuries he has been ground down by oppression. The bad side of his nature has been developed, the good side sadly dwarfed. Do not judge him by the Anglo-Saxon, nineteenth-century standard. He cannot stand it. Be just and you will have more charity. He thirsts for education and he needs the gospel of love. Will you continue to supply this need?"

She told audiences that she looked forward to returning to her work in Van. But according to her obituary, a "trifling fall" close to the time of her planned departure in September 1898 forced her to postpone her plans for one year. In that time complications caused the injury to develop into something more serious. Before her doctors cleared her to return to work, they told her she would require surgery. In order to be certain she was sufficiently recovered in time for departure, the surgery was scheduled for late May 1899. In a letter she wrote to James Rendel Harris on August 29, 1899, Grace Kimball's opinion about the operation was that it was "by no means imperative" and was also "against my advice." But because she wanted to return to her work, KBF decided to go ahead with the surgery.

She entered Carney Hospital, a Catholic centre in Boston, Massachusetts. Though the nature of the injuries resulting from her "trifling fall" in 1898 are not known, KBF, a Presbyterian, chose to enter Boston's first Catholic hospital, run by the Daughters of Charity of St. Vincent de Paul. In its relatively short history (it was built during the American Civil War), the hospital had acquired an excellent reputation for abdominal surgery. Whatever the reason for her surgery, KBF's procedure was proclaimed a success and she progressed well over the first two weeks post-surgery. Her spirits were excellent, her constitution strong. However, on June 7, 1899, two days after her thirty-second birthday, she died suddenly, of a pulmonary embolism. In her August 29 letter to Harris, Grace Kimball said that the embolism was not related to the surgery itself, but regardless, the clot entered "the pulmonary circulation and killed her as by a rifle shot." Kimball continued, "She wrote me the day before the operation, 'I will be all right.' And so it is.... I am so glad she had the rich satisfaction of that just work in France and Bulgaria. It was a great joy to her and filled her with a great sense of achievement."

All secretaries and some members of the American and Woman's mission boards attended her funeral, presided over by Dr. James L. Barton, Secretary of the American Board of Commissioners for Foreign Missions. Rev. Herbert Allen, KBF's friend and colleague in Van, delivered a "loving and appreciative" eulogy that spoke of "her cheerfulness, her consecration and her wonderful moral courage, never refusing any duty that was laid upon her and always doing it well."

Barton spoke directly to KBF's family in his address, hoping to reassure them of what she had accomplished in her short life:

> I wonder if you and the friends in Nova Scotia realize what a strong Christian woman she was. In her work in the mission field under circumstances most trying, she has always evinced a cheerful, hopeful spirit, and has never shrunk from any duty although it were hard and dangerous....
>
> There were nine thousand people on her relief lists, two large schools were conducted by her, two large rooms filled with women were used for fancy work, which she sent to England and sold for the purpose of relief. There were two doctors connected with her relief work, and there were three factories in which men were at work, all under her care. For nearly nine months she continued her labors until the work was completed. Employments were found to those who remained in Bulgaria, but the most of the refugees returned to their homes in Turkey. No one will ever know the number of lives that were saved by her heroic efforts.

In a letter to James Rendel Harris written on July 18, 1900, Barton wrote, "I heartily endorse all you say of her and for her. We find that her sunny, cheerful, hopeful, unselfish character has made deep impression upon many who came in contact with her.... Her father is living at Sherbrook [*sic*] Nova Scotia and his name is John Fraser.... I am sure the father would be pleased to receive the letters of his child, which you have preserved."

Tributes poured in from England, France, Germany, Switzerland, Bulgaria, and Armenia from people who knew Katherine Bell Fraser from her work in Turkey and Bulgaria, including Mayor Zhekov and the British consul for Bulgaria, who wrote of her work in Varna: "She did a man's work with more than a man's capability."

KBF's remains travelled aboard the steamer *La Grande Duchesse* from Boston to Halifax, where the casket was met by her father, her brother Daniel, her sister Tina, and Tina's husband, Reverend Clayton A. Munro. They accompanied the coffin on the last leg of its journey, to Sherbrooke's Riverside Cemetery, where they laid Katherine Bell Fraser to rest on a hillside just below her mother's grave. The British consul's tribute provided the basis for her epitaph still visible on her lichen-riddled headstone: "Doing a man's work with more than a man's capability." Doubtless KBF would have been humbled by the tribute, while heartily approving the choice.

References

In addition to the papers of Katherine Bell Fraser's missionary work in Armenia from 1892–97 in the Nova Scotia Archives (Finding Aid #MGI Vol. 2431–2), the following resources proved very helpful in setting her story in the context of the times in which she lived.

Black, Ros. *A Talent for Humanity: The Life and Work of Lady Henry Somerset*. Chippenham, Wiltshire: Antony Rowe Publishers, 2010.

"Death of Miss Katherine B. Fraser." *Herald* (Yarmouth), no date.

Derengil, Selim. "'The Armenian Question Is Finally Closed': Mass Conversions of Armenians in Anatolia during the Hamidian Massacres of 1895–1897." *Comparative Studies in Society and History* 51(2), (2009): 344–71.

Gifford, Carolyn De Swarte, ed. *Writing Out My Heart: Selections from the Journal of Frances E. Willard 1855–1896*. Urbana: University of Illinois Press, 1995.

Greene, Frederick Davis. *The Armenian Crisis in Turkey: The Massacre of 1894, Its Antecedents and Significance*. London & New York: G.P. Putnam and Sons, 1895.

———. *Armenian Massacres: Or the Sword of Mohammed*. Philadelphia and Chicago: International Publishing Co., 1896.

Hamlin, Cyrus. "The Armenian Massacres," *The Outlook* 52 (December 1895): 944–5.

Howard, William Willard. *Horrors of Armenia: The Story of an Eye-witness*. New York: Armenian Relief Association, 1896.

"A Just Tribute to a Noble Life: The Late Kate B. Fraser, Armenian Missionary." *Chronicle* (Halifax), June 20, 1899.

Knapp, Grace. *The Tragedy of Bitlis*. New York, Chicago, London, and Edinburgh: Fleming H. Revell Company, 1919.

Papers of the Chamberlain Sisters, Beatrice, Ida, Hilda and Ethel Chamberlain, University of Birmingham, Cadbury Research Library, Special Collections, Finding Aid #XBC/A/3/2.

Papers of James Rendel Harris and Helen Balkwill Harris, University of Birmingham, Cadbury Research Library, Special Collections, Finding Aid #XDA21/1/1/26.

"Sherbrooke Village History," sherbrookevillage.novascotia.ca/sites/default/files/inline/documents/history_of_sherbrooke_village.pdf.

Thelberg, Elizabeth B. "An American Heroine in the Heart of Armenia: Dr. Grace Kimball and Her Relief Work in Van." *Review of Reviews* 13 (April 1896): 444–9.

Wilson, Ann Marie. "In the Name of God, Civilization, and Humanity: The United States and the Armenian Massacres of the 1890s." *Le Mouvement Social* 2(2), (2009): 27–44. https://doi.org/10.3917/lms.227.0027.